# UNLOCKED

Access Your Trapped, True Potential To Succeed By Identifying The Godfather Within

Dr KOUSAR A SHAH

# STARDOM BOOKS

## WORLDWIDE

www.StardomBooks.com

**STARDOM BOOKS**

A Division of Stardom Publishing

and infoYOGIS Technologies.

105-501 Silverside Road

Wilmington, DE 19809

Copyright © 2022 by Dr Kousar A Shah

All rights reserved, including right to reproduce
this book or portions thereof in any form whatsoever

# FIRST EDITION JANUARY 2022

## Stardom Books

### UNLOCKED
Access Your Trapped, True Potential To Succeed By Identifying The Godfather Within

Dr Kousar A Shah

p. 219
cm. 13.5 X 21.5

Category:

SEL027000: SELF-HELP / Personal Growth / Success
BUS107000: BUSINESS & ECONOMICS / Personal Success

ISBN-13: 978-1-957456-02-7

# DEDICATION

While penning down this book, I understood how each of us picks up so much from our parents without realizing it. Those learnings construct us and become an integral part of our personality as we grow. While writing this book, I revisited so many childhood memories when my father was very much with me. I felt emotional as I remembered how much he had taught and offered me directly and indirectly. He has been a part of my personality, all through the years, to date.

My father passed away unexpectedly when I was in 12th standard. He was young and a High Court Judge in the State of Jammu & Kashmir. He had earned a tremendous reputation of a staunch honest, disciplined, and principled judge and an exceptional human being. His sudden leaving shocked and devastated us all.

Though it's been more than three decades since his death, there is not a single day when I have not missed him. While writing this book, I came to a different realization. I have realized he has made me the way I am today. My learnings from his life have strengthened my foundation, which has enabled me to ascend the desirable ladders of professional success.

My mother is still with me. Though very old and weak, her very presence continues to support, motivate, encourage, and bless me in countless ways. And for my father, though he is no longer physically present in my life, I still feel his impact every day.

"This book is for you, Daddy. You embodied the truest form of a noble human being with a towering personality, filled with the love of family, devotion to the work, disciplined to the core, and passion for success with no shortcuts. You were well-loved everywhere you served and by every life you touched. As you look down from there, I hope you may feel proud of your most troublesome son as I attempt to guide others through this book."

# CONTENTS

Acknowledgments     i

INTRODUCTION     1

1. INTEGRITY     7
   The Mother of All the Virtues A Leader Must Possess, Is A Choice Between Convenience and What's Right

2. HUMILITY     25
   True Humility Is Thinking Light of Oneself to Go Higher in The Ladder to Success, An Acceptance That You Are Not Always Right, And You Do Not Have All the Answers All the Time

3. COURAGE     43
   Overcoming Fears and Building the Courage, And Grace Under Pressure

4. DILIGENCE & DETERMINATION     59
   Decide. Commit. Succeed

5. DISCIPLINE     77
   A Choice Between Pain of Discipline or Pain of Regret and Failure

6. FOCUS     99
   Channeling Your Energies, And Learning to Ignore Shadows to Hold to Substance

7. RESPONSIBILITY & ACCOUNTABILITY     121
   Gardening Your Soul with Ownership

| 8 | PASSION | 139 |

Chasing Passions and Not Pensions, Keeping the Positive Fire Ignited

| 9 | EYE FOR DETAIL | 159 |

Finding Magic in The Details, And Knowing the Difference Between Mediocrity and Excellence

| 10 | STRONG FOUNDATION | 179 |

Forging Roots to Weather Winds of Change

# ACKNOWLEDGMENTS

To those who bear with me for my psychically workaholic ways of working and support me at times with their silent tolerance or loud words of encouragement, be it my mother, my sister, my brothers, in my early days, or my wife, my daughter, and my son today. All of them help me go on and on, with no undue pressures or demands exerted from their side, and that support is like a path creator for me.

# INTRODUCTION

*"You have abundant dexterity and the power to do such wonderful things in you and it is only you who can bring out the marvelous works within to reality to the awesome amazement of all. You shall always think about them and they shall always be within you until you take steps to make them happen in reality. Awake and do something!"* — Ernest Agyemang Yeboah

It was a wintery night, and the fog flowed across the road. I had to walk down this road as my bike had broken down. I had to park it on the side and walk on the road to find some form of public transport to go home or in the less likely chance find a mechanic's shop. It was not a populated road; hence, only trees or bushes flanked it. However, as I was familiar with the road, I knew it would lead to the main road in a locality where I hoped to find a mechanic or transportation.

Despite the fog, I could see the scattered light from a single street lamp in the distance. It stood out as there was complete darkness around it. I could also make out that the light was flickering; probably, the bulb was at the fag end of its life. I walked towards that distant, flickering, and scattered light. It had become my undeclared destination to reach up and then move further ahead towards my goal.

Suddenly, the light disappeared in a trice. I could not even see a flickering light. I now found myself in pitch dark surroundings with no visibility. It was 1998; hence there were no mobile phones to use as a torch or call someone.

I had no choice in the darkness but to walk, as I could not have found either transportation or a mechanic by staying put. Despite my eyes failing to see anything on that dark night, I had to move ahead and keep walking.

It was a situation I was thrown into, and I still had to find my way. I had to ensure that I remained on the right track and not bump into any trees and bushes or fall into potholes. At that point, I realized my inner eyes were coming forward to help me to find the way. I found my body experiencing everything around it, giving me 360-degree visibility through perceptive powers. I found my feet displaying such dexterity to ensure that I wasn't trapped anywhere and let me stay on the right track. My hands were more like my 'weapon' to safeguard me from hitting anything from the front. My ears were hearing the sounds that I had never realized existed before. My nose could detect any change in smells even as I crossed the trees and bushes emanating their specific scents. To top it all, my mind was exhibiting superhuman control of the situation. I had not known that was my strength. After more than 3 kilometers of this walk in the dark, I reached the market where I wanted to be.

That particular day I realized the power inside me. I never knew it existed inside me in such abundance. And let me tell you, I am not the only person. I am sure all of you must have experienced in some form or the other. You would have discovered how your innermost mind, eyes, and senses came to your rescue when you were in a dark spot. This innermost power is within us, but we seldom use it to its potential.

The same is true of attaining success in life, be it personal or professional. Most of the time, throughout our lives, we keep trying to copy others or keep searching for some help from outside. We mostly look for support in the form of a Godfather. However, we are already carrying this Godfather within, without most of us realizing it. We have this support inside us, but we don't tap it, and we keep searching for others to help us tap our own hidden support, our own innermost Godfather.

Everyone on this planet wants to move upwards; everyone wants to get ahead in life, everyone wants to be successful in whatever the capacity one wants to move ahead, be it as a leader or an entrepreneur. It can be in anything, people want to be successful, but more importantly, they want to remain successful and sustain success.

Somewhat on the same lines, there is an American idea called the American Dream. It was coined by James Truslow Adams when he said, "...*life should be better and richer and fuller for everyone, with opportunity for each according to ability or achievement.*"

So, if there is an American Dream, can there not be an Indian Dream; the dream of a typical Indian? In fact, this dream can be of anyone, irrespective of the country or background or class or race. I believe this is true for any family or person across the globe, be it Indian, American, or any country for that matter. If I could describe it in other words, I would call it a mankind dream!

However, life is never a straight road. You are bound to hit potholes and roadblocks. There will be difficulties to overcome and new challenges to surmount.

One of the challenges would be seeing some people do better than you because they have some form of support or a guide behind them. If you were to look at every person who seems successful, you could imply some form of *jugaad*, (and as we know, the word *jugaad* is owned by our country, which encompasses many meanings under it!) They will have some form of support: their family background, a famous last name, or a Godfather.

This can be disheartening to many people, especially to those who aim to become successful professionals. There will be times when people are promoted because they are well-connected. Being the best performer alone is not enough, people say. They will tell you how you need a good network of people in higher places to ascend. I heard this too. But it did not stop me. It may have affected me, but I knew that I could keep moving ahead, moving up. And so I persevered.

However, some people may be held back by the lack of a support structure. They may take the words of bystanders as facts. They will lament not having a guide or a Godfather to direct them on the correct path. There could be others who are knocked back by one setback and are not able to recover. Some may have regrets about not taking a chance earlier and bemoan the loss of an opportunity. Ask them why they cannot do it anymore, and they will say that they have different responsibilities now. These are the fetters that imprison their mind.

There could be some who hit a glass ceiling and are convinced that they cannot shatter it. They do not have the right family background or a famous last name like Tata or Ambani.

There are so many chains holding them back; one setback leads to another. When people start their careers, they do it with seemingly inexhaustible energy. They are motivated to succeed and reach the greatest heights they can climb.

They have left the nest for the first time. When they were at home, school, or college, they had a support system. They had parents, peers, and teachers to guide them. But that is not the case when they start their careers. They may have to face numerous issues like moving to a new state or country, hyper-competition, and adaptability. There are bound to be setbacks. There will be times when their commitment will be questioned. In the beginning, they will respond to these challenges with verve and vigor. They have the desire to be successful.

That desire and passion will be the fuel that drives them to confront these challenges head-on. The issue becomes severe when they face a few setbacks continually. They might adopt different tactics but meet with nothing but failure. It is at this juncture that they meet the negative spiral of emotions and failure. Doubts will creep in, and they will find it hard to motivate themselves. It will be harder to recover from every fall. Then they will hear the tempting sound of the devil prompting them to take shortcuts to success. Some will take it and find immediate successes.

If they are not caught, they feel empowered to continue taking shortcuts. The devil will whisper that they tried so hard the honest way and look where it got them. If there is a shortcut, why not take it? I have seen many people go down this way. They may think that they are on top of the world, but they are bound to soon come crashing down. The reason is simple: they attempted to build skyscrapers without having the right foundation. I did not have a Godfather, either, and had in fact even lost my father at a very young age.

However, for the last few years I have been in the top leadership positions in healthcare business vertical, and currently being the Group COO at Aakash Healthcare and in a way have been able to realize that Indian dream. In my career, I have come across many people who fell due to the pitfalls I mentioned earlier. I have also mentored many people who found life challenging and lacked any form of a support structure. I also came across people who had a great support structure like a Godfather to guide them. However, most people belong to the former category. The world has changed.

For example, the farmer's son may now be a doctor or an engineer. He cannot look to his father for guidance in his career. When he faces a professional challenge, he cannot look to others as the professional world is hyper-competitive. There is a need to stay ahead of the curve. It is easy to get lost in this pursuit to be successful.

I have written this book for those of you who feel lost. If you have stumbled and are finding it hard to respond to challenges, then this book is for you. I have written this book to tell you that you do not need to look outward for a Godfather. You already possess the greatest support structure. It is within you. You are the answer. You can be the Godfather of your own life and chart the route to your success. The real Godfather is inside all of us.

Look at a successful star professional or entrepreneur – it could be a first-generation businessman or someone who has scaled up the family's enterprise. They all realized that their Godfather was within them.

They fleshed out this Godfather by adding a firm foundation and certain core values. Some people have achieved success by using dishonest means. But they can never sustain that success. I have written this book because I found my inner Godfather. I have been able to stay successful. I came across many people who failed to sustain their success. Sustainable success is a different ball game. It was Bruce Springsteen who said, *"Getting an audience is hard. Sustaining an audience is hard. It demands a consistency of thought, of purpose, and of action over a long period of time."* While Bruce Springsteen was speaking of how to be successful as a musician, I believe it translates well across any profession. I have written this book to help you be consistent in thought, purpose, and action.

I was fortunate to have had some excellent role models in life. The way they lived their lives taught me invaluable lessons. I have learned from them that life's challenges are big learning opportunities. Every setback is a chance to evolve and grow. I took the lessons I learned from them to build the foundation from which I could soar into the skies. There are people who can tell you the secrets of flying high, but I want to impress upon you the importance of building the right base through this book. You can read any number of self-help books and listen to motivational speakers to give that momentary thrust of energy. But if you want to attain sustainable success, you need to unveil your inner Godfather.

It is your inner Godfather who will provide you the resilience when you need it the most. However, if you need to unveil your inner Godfather, you need to have the right foundation. I have written this book to help you do just that. I want to stress that you need to become a good human before you become a successful one. You can even see this in some leaders. As they ascend the ladder of hierarchy, they become different. They lose sight of their humanity. It is important that you also grow as a human being as you climb the ladder of success. These qualities go hand-in-hand. Every quality you need to cultivate to be successful will also help you become a better human being.

# 1
# INTEGRITY
**The mother of all the virtues a leader must possess, is a choice between convenience and what's right**

*"Honesty is the first chapter in the book of wisdom."* —Thomas Jefferson

**Bundle of Temptation**

It was late in the night. A man stretched out his hand and extended a bundle of Rs 500 notes to me. I noticed that he appeared to be really distressed about something. Well, his daughter's life was on the line, in a literal sense. But before you take any wrong leaps of imagination, I should probably tell you the whole story.

This incident occurred during one of my night duties in 1997 when I was a houseman in the department of Pediatrics. I got called to the Emergency Department for a very sick baby who had come in and I had rushed to see the child. I did all that was needed to stabilize the child clinically and admitted her to the Emergency Ward. Following this, I completed all the necessary clinical work, including the documentation, gave the necessary treatment-related instructions to the nurses, and stepped out into the corridor. As I was walking back to the duty doctors' room, I heard someone calling out. I turned around to see the child's father crying inconsolably. I immediately went back, and spoke to him, and shared the clinical condition of his daughter. I explained the procedures that were carried out and what he could expect.

I was trying to motivate him to stay positive. Suddenly he held my hand and put a bundle of notes in it. I could see the notes were in the denomination of Rs 500 each. He told me, "Doctor sir, please keep this money and see that you reserve your best treatment for my daughter." I was stunned. I pushed the bundle back into his hands and told him, "Sir, this is a government hospital. You need not spend a single rupee here. We will treat your daughter to the best of our capabilities, no matter what." He tried pushing the bundle back and said, "This is for your expense, sir. Do not worry. I will not share this with anybody else." I was enraged by his remarks. I threatened to call the cops on him for trying to bribe me. He was taken aback by my reaction. He immediately fell at my feet, apologized, picked up the money, and left.

But when I completed my shift, the incident replayed itself in my mind. For some reason, I was unable to rest easy. I did not know why. Certain vagrant thoughts led me to question my decision to refuse that amount of money. The silver-tongued devil was whispering in my ear, the many things I could have done with that money. Even as my thoughts were running rampant about the possibilities, I shivered

It was as if my whole body rejected this opportunity. My wild thoughts immediately quietened down, and I was reminded of my father. There is an adage that talks about a clear conscience making a good pillow. I slept well that night. I had no other thoughts as I knew that I had done the right thing. I had inculcated the virtues of honesty and integrity from my father without my knowing. The very same virtues that I had doubts about had become a part of my make-up. I understood the mindset of that child's father, but through this incident, I was able to connect with my father and realize that the monetary compensation did not decide the value of my work and my life. It was about doing my job sincerely and honestly to the best of my ability.

## A Father's Legacy

I remember this day as if it happened yesterday. I was fresh from college and doing my housemanship in a government hospital in Delhi. I loved going to work every day with boundless energy. I did not mind the hours as I saw it as an opportunity to hone my skill and enhance my knowledge in my chosen subject, pediatrics.

I saw every patient who came to consult me as a fresh learning opportunity as every new case had something to teach me. I never turned away a patient during my working hours. You could say I was a happy-go-lucky young doctor who was only concerned about being good at his job. Whenever I had time off, I spent it with my wife, where we went on dates and planned our future. Other off-times were spent in the company of my friends where we had fun doing various activities. So, my life revolved around my work and having fun in the company of my friends and family. During this time, my honesty and integrity were never put to the test. So, these crucial values never figured in my mind.

If you were to ask me, I would have never known that my moral foundation was built on the values of honesty and integrity. As I said before, I was a doctor whose days were filled with hospital duties or fun times with my wife and friends. I never took the time to introspect and understand what made me, me. However, as time passed and I began to introspect, I could trace that my moral foundations were laid from observing my father. He lived his life according to a strict moral code.

His behavior and life had influenced me subconsciously to such an extent that I never realized that the so-called big virtues like honesty and integrity had been ingrained so deeply in the foundations of my make-up. There was a point in my childhood when I used to wonder about my father's strict adherence to living an honest life with the highest integrity. This thought struck me as he had received numerous direct or indirect 'offers.' He refused them all. However, I used to think there was nothing wrong with taking some monetary compensation for a favor. It was an especially striking thought as I saw the rest of the world do the same. Why was my father not being part of something that was already accepted and practiced by others?

However, even without my realizing it, these virtues were embedded in my foundation somewhere. The first time I ever realized this was when the father of that child offered me a bribe to take care of his child better, and I felt vehemently repulsed by it.

*"Where there is righteousness in the heart, there is beauty in the character. When there is beauty in the character, there is harmony in the home. When there is harmony in the home, there is order in the nation. When there is order in the nation, there is peace in the world."* – A. P. J. Abdul Kalam

**Honesty at the Workplace**

If you want to be successful in any profession or vocation, you need to possess good character. If you are dishonest, you may get away with it once or twice or maybe even a few times. But your dishonesty is sure to catch up with you one day. You can cultivate a good character by simply practicing honesty and integrity. It may not seem appealing now as we are in an era of instant gratification. You may even know of many people who made something out of their lives by taking a shortcut or two. It can be incredibly tempting to take one shortcut and think that you can get away with it. That very thought should warn you of the wrong path. Work toward building a mentality that says this path is wrong instead of one that says you will not get caught.

You may not reap the fruits of honesty immediately. It may not even be realized the next day or any time soon. Persevere, for if you do so, success will find you. Such success will also not be transient. I am sure you have heard of how you need one lie to cover another lie.

This phrase puts it aptly—To hide a lie, a thousand lies are needed. When you take shortcuts, you will either be caught or be dissatisfied. That dissatisfaction can be traced to your conscience, which knows that you took the wrong way. Thus, you will either find yourself stuck in a rut of regret or find yourself in a loop running away.

You will be stuck pursuing the next high from a successful endeavor to tamp down the dissatisfaction. However, as you seek such success to quiet your disquiet mind and not for success itself, you will again look to take shortcuts. You will look for such shortcuts as you crave that temporary elation from success to silence your unease quickly.

So, you will constantly be chasing the next peak with no time to reflect on your learnings and success. Such joy is always tainted and ephemeral. But when you are successful due to the strength of your character, it will be yours and cannot be easily taken away from you. Your moral strength will be woven into the fabric of your life, and you can bravely face the storms of desire and greed. The success you earn in life based on your values will be that much more valuable to you.

## Leading with Integrity

Let us take an example. Let us suppose you have a boss. He is friendly and his project completion rate is among the highest in the company. However, there are rumors that he is slightly unscrupulous. He has no qualms when it comes to pushing his subordinates to post numbers that he finds satisfactory. He is also known to go to any extreme to keep his numbers constant and high. Now, let us take another example of a boss. He is a bit more sober in his interactions and relationships with others. However, he has a clean reputation for doing things the right way. He may not be as successful in terms of numbers as the former boss was, but he is a high-performing leader. Who would you like to work under? It is obvious that the second person would be a better leader. He will be honest, and he will expect you to be honest as well. You will know that such a leader will be honest in his feedback and praise.

Let us flip the situation. What type of leader do you want to be? If you are the second type of leader, more people will want to follow you. When you are a person of integrity, people will be attracted to you. They will find comfort in your honesty and professionalism. You will gain the trust of the people around you. They could be your colleagues, team members, bosses, friends, and even family members. When you are true to your character, you help build an environment that encourages others to be the same. You will become a role model, and this only augurs well for you in the long run.

*"One of the truest tests of integrity is its blunt refusal to be compromised."* – Chinua Achebe

I remember another incident in my initial days as a hospital administrator in 2005. I got a call from the reception informing me that one of the attendants of a patient was causing a huge ruckus in the hospital. Several people tried to talk to him. The nurses, doctors, and even other managers tried reasoning with him. But he only seemed to be getting angrier by the minute. I was called as I was the Assistant Medical Superintendent. I asked the staff to escort him to my office. He stormed in and almost deafened me with the decibel of his voice. I could see that he was enraged. I asked him to sit, and I listened.

I allowed him to speak his mind and listened to his concerns. I learned that his name was Dheeraj. I traced the root cause of his complaint after listening to him. There seemed to be some miscommunication between the doctor who was looking after the patient and Dheeraj. Dheeraj was distressed, and he had sought some clarity from the hospital staff. He tried to approach other people to find out if the doctor had committed any mistake. However, the staff did not take kindly to that insinuation. Thus, whenever Dheeraj met anyone, they all tried to deny any error rather than provide any clarity.

As soon as I realized the problem, I apologized to him. I knew that we were at fault. We had not provided any clarity to him. As soon as he heard the apology, I could visibly see that he had calmed down. He was acknowledged finally. The apology comforted him greatly. I gave him some more time to catch his breath. Then I offered to mediate a discussion with the concerned doctor to address the communication gap. He gladly accepted my offer. So, I had the concerned doctor come to my office.

The three of us had a discussion where we resolved the issues. It was quite a sight to see the two parties who were shouting at each other earlier shaking their hands at the end of the discussion. The three of us then had a good cup of coffee with much warmer dispositions toward each other. Dheeraj would become my friend after that incident and is still a good friend to this day. In a later conversation, he admitted that my honesty helped him mellow down that day.

On a trying day, under extenuating circumstances, it was my honesty that got through to him. What can we learn from that story? I could repeat the childhood adage that honesty is the best policy. But there is a reason that such a phrase became an adage. From my interaction with Dheeraj, it can be seen that you can conquer any form of negativity with honesty. It can be quite disarming.

*"The wind might cause a kite to rise, but what keeps it up there is the fact that somebody on the ground has a steady hand. You have to hold steady to your values - your integrity. It's your anchor. You let go of that... well, it isn't long before your kite comes crashing down."* – Mark Victor Hansen and Robert G. Allen

## Always Do the Right Thing

One of the first lessons I learned about integrity was from my father. I was a teenager, and I was learning how to ride a motorcycle, way back in 1988-89. My elder brother had a bike, and as was typical of boys my age, I wanted to ride it. But I was still in the process of obtaining a driving license.

Hence, my father did not permit me to ride the bike outside the official bungalow boundaries. I was upset with my father. I tried a variety of methods. I tried to coax him and even went to the extent of giving him the cold shoulder to change his mind. He was unmoved. My antics did not budge him, and this frustrated me further. This frustration boiled over one day, and I asked him furiously why he was so obstinate. He said that I did not possess a driving license. I argued that I could ride the bike, and no one needed to know that I had no driving license. But my father was clear. He said, "Son, it is not whether someone knows or watches you ride a bike without a driving license. Others may or may not know, but one person knows and that person is you. Remember that you are always a witness to all your deeds. And the issue here is that you will be committing a wrong deed. In this case, it is also illegal. Just ask yourself if you did ride the bike without the license, would it be wrong?" He waited for me to nod my assent that it would be a bad deed. Then he continued, "Son, whether someone knows or sees should not influence your actions. Make sure that you are convinced you are doing the right thing, and do not do things you know are wrong. When you do the right thing even when nobody is watching, it is a mark of your character."

While I did grumble away as a teenager, I only realized the value of that incident later on in my life. At that moment, I learned something from my father through opposition and disagreement. Work on such increments daily. Such small incidents in my life and the discussions and debates with my father shaped my life and built my character. These small building blocks of integrity meant that when I faced that parent of the child who offered me a bundle of cash, I knew the right thing to do. So, work on building your life with such small habits of integrity. They will slowly reflect in your personality. When you reflect such positive vibes, people will feel them. We feel the positive vibes of a person when they are strong in their character.

When they have a strong character, positivity oozes out of them. You, too, can exude such positivity and affect people positively when you cultivate your character by adhering to the virtues of honesty and integrity. The quicker you realize that being true to yourself is the greatest gift you can give yourself, the better. There are many who can be brutally honest with the world and the people around them. However, they do not offer the same luxury to themselves. They live in constant denial of themselves. They find it hard to face themselves and constantly put themselves down.

They are a mess internally as they know that they do not fit the disguise they have donned. It is an itch that refuses to go away. If they spend too long denying the truth about themselves, they may become numb to that irritation. However, they will never be at peace. It will always gnaw on their psyche and even the successes they achieve will feel inadequate.

When such people assume a leadership position, the end result will probably be an unhealthy work culture. Such leaders will be problematic to the team, to the organization, and to themselves as well. They will be driven by feelings of inadequacy and will tend to compromise when it comes to making a stand.

## A Desirable Work Culture

Leaders need to be honest and inspire a culture of integrity. Let us say, we have a leader who struggles with being honest in giving feedback. One team member keeps making mistakes. However, the leader is not able to step up and call the person out and point out the mistake. They would rather keep forgiving and overlooking the mistakes to avoid the confrontation that honesty would bring. When the other team members find out about this, they will lose any motivation to be diligent in their work as they have found their leader to be a pushover. They will know that they can get away with sub-standard work.

Here are some of the reasons why leaders must practice honesty and integrity:

1. **You reflect what is inside you:** You may don many guises and wear different looks. They may be of different hues and varying contrasts. However, if these are not the projection of your true personality, your disguise will be found out.

People will know that it is a false representation of your personality. These colors may dazzle momentarily, but once the sheen wears off, you will be left with the grotesqueness of the mauling you have left on yourself. Nothing lasts forever and nothing stays the same. However, there is one exception that stands the test of time. It is the truth. You may tell a lie today for a short-term gain. However, it will return to haunt you. So, if you want anything to last forever, it has to be authentic, true, and honest. So, stay true to who you are and you will last longer. When you stay true to yourself, you will also discover your hitherto hidden self-worth. As a leader, when you have pride in yourself, you will extend the same courtesy to your team members as well. When leaders are not honest with themselves, they will have an inferior view of themselves. Consequently, they will turn the same inferior gaze on their team as well.

2. **You become more courageous:** When you are honest with yourself, you become more accepting of yourself. You do not berate yourself over your flaws and weaknesses. When you are honest with yourself, you also know your strengths and capabilities. Being honest with yourself is not the same as self-pity or self-loathing. It is about having a holistic picture of yourself and accepting it. When you know yourself thus, the opinions of others will not be barbs that will hurt you. You will not be affected by other people's opinions of you as you know who you are, better than anyone else. Having this mindset will help you overcome any apprehensions you might have about what others may think or say. You will stop worrying about how it would depict you and only look at how you can do a certain activity and improve.

3. **You have healthier relationships:** When you are honest with yourself, you remove a burden from your relationships. When we are not honest with ourselves, we look outward to our relationships to provide us the worth and esteem that we cannot provide for ourselves. This can be taxing on any relationship and will burden the other person to pull more weight in that relationship.

This is not an example of a healthy relationship. When you are not honest with yourself, you start being dishonest in your relationships as well. You will be more worried about how you seem than being who you are. If a relationship has to thrive and stand the test of time, the other person has to know the real you and not the 'you' that you want to reveal.

4. **You lead a better life:** This is a consequence of the aforementioned three points. When you are not stressed with images and labels, you shed the disguise that you had forced yourself to wear to have a positive image in public. When you live your life dictated by public opinion, you will wear clothes that you do not like and speak in tongues that you do not favor. If you notice, this would become the mantra for your life. You would be living a life that is not of your choosing. Such a life can be stressful. Like the proverbial sword of Damocles, you will have the constant fear of discovery and rejection hanging over you. When you are honest with yourself, you accept yourself. Public opinion cannot shake you. You would have gotten rid of one of your greatest burdens. You will realize you do not need to bear the cross of public opinion. Only your opinion matters, and when you are truly honest with yourself, your opinion will be that of acceptance and joy. When you come across this realization, you will lead a far more plentiful, happy, and productive life.

One may think that honesty and integrity can be tough tasks. It is certainly easier to lie and get away than to say the truth and face the consequences. The consequences of telling the truth can be bitterly painful sometimes, but the consequences you may face when your lie is exposed can be far worse.

However, there is not much cause for concern as cultivation of these traits is not as difficult as it seems. Self-honesty starts from, well, self. You need to face yourself and remove the masks you have worn for others' benefit. Face yourself and you may not like who looks back at you. However, I can assure you there can be no sight more beautiful. When you look at yourself honestly without the filters of pity, anger, and loathing, you will find yourself open, warm, and vulnerable.

This may not be easy initially, but if you steel yourself to take an honest look at yourself, you will find who you truly are. If you feel you need someone else's help, rely on someone you can trust to help you face yourself.

We can rely on the tool used by businesses to examine themselves and their position in the world.

## Self-SWOT Analysis

Businesses rely on SWOT (Strengths, Weaknesses, Opportunities, Threats) to find out their actual position in the market and how they can move to realize their competitive advantage. We too can use the SWOT analysis to help figure out who we are and how we can move forward. So, create a table on a sheet of paper or you may also use an Excel document. List out columns under the headings of Strengths, Weaknesses, Opportunities, and Threats. It is essential that you write it or type it out. It is a sign of the commitment you hold to develop this trait. When you have this in black and white, you will find that you are able to plan better and be open and more honest with yourself.

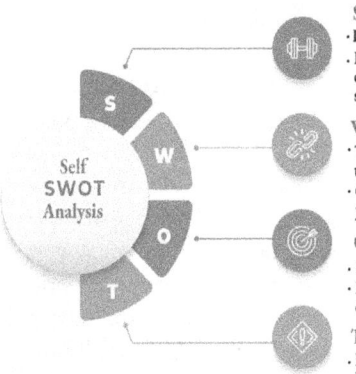

**STRENGTHS**
· List anything that you feel you are good at.
· It could be a talent like singing or a personal capability where people trust you with their secrets, etc.

**WEAKNESSES**
· The first step in addressing a problem is to identify it.
· Once you have identified your weaknesses, you can then draw up plans to counter them.

**OPPORTUNITIES**
· List a few personal chances that you wish to take.
· List areas where you can fill in with training or education.

**THREATS**
· Identify the roadblocks and challenges that can be surpassed through effort and planning.

## Strengths

List anything that you feel you are good at. It could be a talent like singing, or a technical skill like proficiency in computer programming or coding.

It could be a personal capability where people trust you with their secrets, etc. Just list the activities you excel at. Recall your greatest moments of triumph and success. Did you give a successful presentation? Were you lauded for your skill in mathematics when you won a competition? Have you been commended for your patience and listening skills? These will give you an idea of where your strengths lie.

**Weaknesses**

I know this can be tough as no one likes to acknowledge their weaknesses. It would help to think that having a weakness is not an indictment of who you are. The first step in addressing a problem is to identify it. Hence, it is critical that you know your weaknesses. When you list down your weaknesses, you will know the areas that need improvement in your life.

This section is critical as this is the section that holds the greatest potential for self-development. Thus, I cannot stress this enough, you need to be as brutally honest and truthful as you can in this section. Do not shy away or feel embarrassed. This section will highlight what needs focus in your life. You can list bad habits or fears. Are you scared of public speaking? Do you struggle to retain your focus in a meeting? Do you lack a technical certification? Honesty in this segment is a sign of self-awareness.

Once you have identified your weaknesses, you can then draw up plans to counter them. I would like to recount an episode from my life. When he was young, my son had a terrible fear of dogs. Even the bark of a dog would make him shudder. He used to be wary of walking on roads when there were stray dogs present. He would always walk slowly and carefully on the roads.

Sometimes, I would notice the fear on his face when a dog barked from a couple of streets over. I thought about this for a while. I decided on a plan of action and broached the topic with him. I asked him if he would like to adopt a puppy. I thought that having a friendly puppy of his own would help him get over his fear of dogs. He liked my idea and agreed to have a puppy. Accordingly, in February 2019, we adopted a 40-day-old German Shepherd pup. My son was ecstatic, and slowly as the puppy grew, his fear of dogs also started to melt away. Today, two years later, the puppy is a big dog and my son has forgotten that he used to be afraid of dogs.

## Opportunities

This section is primarily geared toward identifying professional opportunities. You could list a few personal chances that you wish to take as well. List areas where you can fill in with training or education. Is there a course or certification that will help you get a promotion or raise? Will attending a workshop provide you with networking for closing a deal? Is there a new job available that would be perfect for you? Do you think you are lagging in certain technical competencies that can be resolved via training? Will a certain educational degree help you progress further in your career? These are the questions that you need to answer in this segment.

## Threats

You will identify the roadblocks on your path. The difference between this section and the section 'Weaknesses' is that you are dealing with external sources in this segment. They could be your colleagues, your college degrees or the lack thereof, your profile, etc. These are the challenges that can be surpassed through effort and planning. Once you have a SWOT analysis of yourself, you can then plan on how to leverage your strengths and utilize your opportunities to overcome your weaknesses and threats. This exercise will help you be honest with yourself and help you become more accepting as well.

## Developing Integrity

However, how can we develop our integrity? It might seem difficult; however, there are many instances in our daily life that can provide us with this opportunity.

1. **Live up to your words.** Your word has to be your bond. When you give a verbal commitment, ensure that you fulfill it. If you wish to be trustworthy and reliable to your family, to your colleagues, and, crucially, to yourself, follow through on your promises. Your words should carry the weight of your personality. When you do not fulfill your promises or word, they will lose their value. I would remind you of the story of the boy who cried 'wolf.' One day, your voice will also become meaningless if you cannot stand behind them.

If there is a genuine reason for your failure to keep your promise, ensure that you apologize and let the concerned people know of it directly from you. Assure them and ensure that it does not become a pattern.

2. **Stick to your appointments.** In a similar vein, keep your appointments. They are a mark of your professionalism and trustworthiness.

3. **Think before you make a commitment.** To ensure that your words are valuable, take your time. Consider the commitment you wish to make before you make it. Take a pause and evaluate. Ask yourself if you can do it. Remember, when you make a commitment to deliver, you are committing to do it to the best of your ability. Do not make promises if you are going to be punctual at the cost of compromised quality. Hence, take your time and consider all these aspects before you make a commitment.

4. **Be comfortable to say a NO.** Some people can be burdened by refusal. They assume that saying no would reflect poorly on them. If you are such a person, it would be best to remember that it would reflect even more poorly on you, if you were to say yes, and then either fail to deliver or underperform. No effective leader will say yes to everything that comes their way. Become comfortable with saying no when you feel that you cannot deliver on a commitment. Be polite in your refusal.

5. **Mind your knee-jerk reactions.** One surefire way to fail is to be impulsive. When you are impulsive, you are reactive. This is a regressive way of living. Imagine a chess game. Why are some people good at it and others not? The best chess players win because they can think many moves ahead. Their moves are not dictated by each move of the opponent. Knee-jerk reactions are signs of muddle-headed thinking. They point to a lack of clear strategy. Take time to reflect on your impulsive decisions in the past. What could you have done better?

6. **Your communication skills define you.** Think before you speak. Know that your words represent you and your organization. This is especially true when you interact with people who do not know you personally. Therefore, mind your words when you speak or write an e-mail. Rethink and reread your words before you communicate with others.

7. **Think of some habits and skills to enhance your integrity.** Do you tend to speak ill of others behind their backs? Do you indulge in gossip? What are some of your other habits that you do not want people to know about? My barometer is to do only what I would do openly in front of others. For example, If I am speaking of someone in their absence, I will only talk about those things that I would in their presence. If I have an issue with someone, I address it with them directly and not with others. This is true integrity, and it will always be your strength. Let me remind you of this old saying—He who talks to you about others, talks to others about you!

8. **Avoid people with low integrity.** This is self-evident. You are the company you keep. Avoid people who are dishonest and lack integrity. Even if you are spotless, your association with such people will cast a shadow over you.

If you wish to work on your honesty and integrity, know that it takes commitment and effort on a daily basis. I have drawn up an exercise to help you on that count. Work on the exercise that is based on what I have said earlier in the chapter. You can also devise tools of your own to develop your honesty and integrity.

| | | |
|---|---|---|
| Find Your Godfather Inside You | Honesty & Integrity | Write Here |
| Learning Exercise | Recall incidents where you believe your honesty or integrity was tested by a situation | |
| | Remember how you had responded | |
| | Make an honest self-assessment of your response & rank it on a scale of 1–10 | |
| | Now imagine how you would like to respond to the same if given a second chance, or in an ideal scenario to attain 10/10 on the self-score of Honesty and Integrity | |
| | In your self-assessment if you had scored anywhere less than 10, what habit would you like to practice to make it a 10 in future | |

|  | Practice the decided habit daily in the following manner |  |
|---|---|---|
|  | Follow-up for practice of the decided habit thrice daily for 10 days – morning, afternoon, night |  |
|  | Follow-up for practice of the decided habit twice daily for 10 days – morning, night |  |
|  | Follow-up for practice of the decided habit once daily for 10 days, at night |  |

# 2
# HUMILITY

True humility is thinking light of oneself to go higher in the ladder to success, an acceptance that you are not always right, and you do not have all the answers all the time

**Too Much Pride Leads to Destruction**

The fall of many great empires and men can be traced to their pride. The legend of Icarus and Daedalus is a good example. In Greek mythology, Daedalus was renowned as a master architect and craftsman who lived in Athens. He is said to have been a skilled carpenter and inventor and is credited with the designing of many of the carpentry tools in use today. He was a master sculptor as well, and his creations were so life-like that people often mistook them for the real thing. He was very proud of his skills and could not bear the thought of a rival. His sister sent her young son Perdix to learn from Daedalus as an apprentice. He soon noticed that his nephew was equally talented in inventing and designing new products. Daedalus started envying his nephew's popularity, and in a fit of jealousy, threw him down from the Acropolis in Athens to murder him. For this crime, Daedalus was banished from Athens.

He found refuge in the Kingdom of Crete under King Minos. He continued his work as a craftsman and furthered his reputation.

However, he soon created some mischief and got into trouble with the King. King Minos imprisoned Daedalus and his son Icarus in a tall tower for life. Daedalus knew he had to come up with an ingenious plan if both he and his son had to escape from there. He came up with the idea of making a pair of wings for himself and his son. He set to work using the feathers of birds, wax, and some string. The wings were soon ready. Before attempting to fly off the tower, Daedalus cautioned his son. He said that flying too high would cause the wax to melt and the wings would come apart, and flying too low, close to the ocean, would cause the wings to get wet from the foam and spray of the waves and become too heavy to fly. Then the father and son took to the skies from the tower. They were exhilarated by their flight to freedom. When he looked below from on high, Icarus felt like a God.

He forgot his father's warnings and ascended higher and higher into the sky. He felt invincible. Daedalus watched his son fly higher with growing horror. Soon, the wax that held the wings together melted in the sun's heat and the feathers fell away one by one and Icarus plunged to his death.

Here, we see the tale of two men who were too proud of their accomplishments. Daedalus was unwilling to share his popularity and renown with his nephew and this led to his banishment from Athens. Icarus felt he was invincible and would not listen to his father's warning, thereby losing his life.

Humility is a virtue that is not prized enough today. In a world dominated by social media, there seems to be an increasing need to stand out from the crowd. And the easiest way to do this is to be loud and ostentatious. I only learned the importance of humility after a tragic incident in my life.

**The Person Provides Dignity to the Position; Not Vice-versa**

As I mentioned in the previous chapter, my father played a crucial role in shaping me into the man I am today. My father was a judge in the Jammu and Kashmir High Court. As part of the perks of his job, we were provided with house helpers, drivers, and caretakers.

As children, my siblings and I enjoyed the attention we received due to my father's position and role. Many dignitaries and VIPs visited and greeted my father. Even the local people of repute visited us during festivals to meet and greet my father.

As I grew older and left the protective nest of my parents, I began to see the world in a different color. From a slightly cynical perspective, I began to think that those visits and greetings were marks of respect paid to the chair that he held and not to my father himself.

The world did not disabuse me of that view. That perspective was challenged after my father's death. I secured admission to a medical college. By some strange twist of fate, the college happened to be in the same state where my father had presided as the High Court judge. However, with his passing, we were not going to be accorded the same benefits. I was back in the same state where I was once treated like a prince.

I did not expect people to pay attention to me as my father had already departed from this world. However, I was shocked to find people reaching out to me with their care and concern. They took it upon themselves to enquire about my well-being. Perhaps I was treated with greater care and respect than I had been when I was a small child.

One fine day in 1990, I was most surprised when I answered a knock at my hostel door. Two people, Om Prakash and Avatar, were standing there. They were our former house helpers who were assigned to us by the State Government when my father was alive. I was so happy to see them. I used to be a very carefree and reckless child. The moment I saw them, I could not help but extend my arms and hug them. They were reserved and did not want me to behave with such exuberance. But they had been a part of my life, and I could not control my joy.

I thanked them for taking the time to meet me. They then told me that they had come not just to pay a courtesy visit, but to find how they could be of help. When I was a child, I had been pampered, and even chores like washing my clothes were done by the house helpers. They told me that they knew that this task would be difficult for me. They saw some of my scattered clothes in the room. Despite my protests, they gathered all my scattered clothes to wash them. They washed the clothes and returned them to me. I tried to pay them for their work, but they refused point-blank to accept any money.

When I tried to insist, Om Prakash told me, "You do not know what your father meant to us and what he has done for us. He respected us, and never once did he make us feel small.

He was genuine, warm, and open to us. He never let us experience any difference or gap in the hierarchical status. He was that noble. What we have done for you today is nothing. Please take it as our tribute to your wonderful father's soul for his grace, nobility, and humility."

This incident awakened me and filled my heart with gratitude. It also reminded me that I, too, needed to live my life with the same commitment as my father once did. It almost felt like my inner Godfather was prodding me to realize how my father had lived his life and how his legacy would enduringly live on through the people whose lives he had impacted. Om Prakash and Avatar were not alone. I met many more people who just wanted to extend their courtesy and helping hands. When I spoke with them, they all seemed to sing from the same hymn sheet.

They talked of their utmost respect for my father. They could not stop waxing lyrical about how grounded he was and how he never let the authority of his position go to his head. I spoke with the dignitaries and even the seemingly humble staff. They all spoke of their respect and affection toward my father. My father never discriminated against any person. He did his best to help anyone who knocked on his door. Some people even told me of how he had guided them onto the correct path many times. So many of these stories were eye-openers for me. I was not even aware of some of these incidents. My father was never one for publicizing his good deeds. That is when I realized, the respect that they had paid to my father was not for the chair but the man himself.

Some of the senior doctors even pitched in to help with my college education. Medical textbooks were expensive, and people knew that our financial condition was not very stable. These people also knew that my father had never exploited his position for personal gain despite being offered many opportunities. These doctors came forward and provided me with the textbooks for my MBBS course. They refused to take it back and said that this was their form of support. They insisted that this action paled in comparison to the support my father had given them during their time of need.

Let us first examine the word humility. What does it mean? The 1988 edition of the Chambers English Dictionary defines it thus—
*n. the state or quality of being humble: lowliness of mind: modesty: humble, adj. low: lowly: modest: unpretentious: having a low opinion of oneself.*

So, does humility mean having a low opinion of oneself? In short, the answer is no. However, let us ignore the semantics of the word. In this chapter, I want to focus on one aspect listed in the dictionary definition. It is the aspect of modesty. I shall cite one of the most influential novelists of the 20th century, C.S. Lewis. He said, *"Humility is not thinking less of yourself, it's thinking of yourself less."*

There are countless examples of people who fell victim to their hubris. Contrastingly, there are also many examples of how people have been successful because of their humility.

History relegates the former to the scrap heap of what-ifs and immortalizes the latter in time. Let me pick two of the most popular examples. I will take one from the field of sports and another from Bollywood. These are two of the most aspired professions in this country. Many people try to become successful either in Bollywood or in the game of cricket.

It goes without saying that more of them fail than succeed. Only a handful of people actually succeed. If we were to trace the cause for most failures, you would find that almost all these people failed to rein in their ego. They thought of themselves as stars even before they became one. They behaved as such and assumed an attitude that far belied their status. When they tried to assume a lofty status, they lost connection with their roots.

One's attitude is an important aspect of one's personality. If you were to take an informal poll of the people around you, you would find that, given a choice to be somebody either in cricket or in Bollywood, the majority would want to become a Sachin Tendulkar or an Amitabh Bachchan. Why? Is it because of their lofty status? Is it because of their success and longevity? These are all important factors. However, the primary factor would be because they can relate to them better.

Amitabh Bachchan has acted out fantastic scripts, and Sachin has scripted his own fantastical stories with his willow. Yet, they have remained grounded through both their successes and apparent failures. They were not out to flash their accomplishments. They stayed true and honest to their craft and remained humble in the face of incessant praise. It is that humility that appeals to the common man more than the flash and parade. It makes them relatable. However, this is not something unique to these two fields alone. It is true across any field. Look at any inspirational leader across history.

They inspired people through their actions and were extraordinarily humble even when they did extraordinary deeds. Mahatma Gandhi, Nelson Mandela, and Martin Luther King Jr. are all examples of great visionaries.

They inspired people and led revolutionary movements that altered the course of history. Yet, they remained humble in the face of it. If you want to inspire the people around you, you cannot go wrong by following their example. Remember the adage, *"If you want to judge a person's heart, watch how they behave with someone below them or with a subordinate"*. It would be best to keep this in mind always and act accordingly with people. Do not let the chair dictate your actions.

**Handling Success**

Attaining success and remaining successful are two different things. You achieve success due to your effort and will. But sometimes, that success can make you complacent. If you indulge in the sideshows that accompany your success, you may become blind to your faults. You may fail to recognize opportunities to better yourself.

To remain successful, you need to continue being disciplined and alert. You must be willing to learn constantly. You can only do this if you are humble. When you are humble, you will not be taken in by your success. You will ignore the praises that come down from the rafters. You will focus on the road ahead and on how you can stay successful.

Leaders will only be valued when they are successful. Thus, leaders must learn to handle success with humility. When leaders are humble, people will find them approachable. When leaders are approachable, they will know the ground realities of what their team faces. Sometimes, instead of being humble, leaders are so egotistical of their position that they are in danger of getting intoxicated by the rarefied atmosphere they live in up in the clouds, so to speak. It is then that they forget the realities of the world as Icarus once did.

People tend to respect humble leaders more as they are more respectful and honest. How do you identify a good leader? Find out what is being said about them behind their backs. Good leaders are respected and remembered fondly even in their absence. Inevitably, such leaders are respected because they are humble. I must add that one must remain humble in the truest sense.

If you fake being humble, you will be found out quickly. Do not be humble for the sake of appearing to be so. Be humble because you know that there is more to do, and you are not omniscient or omnipotent.

When you have laid the strongest foundations, you can build up to the skies. There is this remarkable story that I stumbled upon. Arthur Ashe is one of the legendary players in tennis history.

He was the first African-American man to win the singles title at Wimbledon, the US Open, and the Australian Open. In 1983, he was diagnosed to be HIV positive; it is believed he contracted HIV due to a blood transfusion during one of his two heart surgeries. He kept the information private until 1992.

When the world came to know about his illness, many people sent him messages and letters with their prayers and regards. One common question he was asked was why God had chosen him to bear that illness. This was Ashe's reply: "*All over the world, some million teenagers aspire to become tennis players. Out of these millions, maybe a hundred thousand reach to some sort of proficiency. Of them, only a few thousand play in some circuit, and only a hundred or so play the grand slam. Finally, only two reach the final of Wimbledon.*

*When I was standing with the trophy of Wimbledon in my hand, I never questioned God, Why Me? And now what right do I have to ask God, Why Me?*"[1]

It is easy to get lost in the trappings of success. When you are successful, people will shower you with extravagant praise. They will show you the utmost respect and affection. Regardless of you being humble, most people will do it because of your authority and influence. Most often, they do it because they expect something in return. They will be, as the popular expression goes, fair-weather friends. There are many examples to demonstrate how once-successful people suddenly lost their adoring masses when they encountered an unfortunate setback. They become shocked and heartbroken seeing this desertion by their friends. They only experience this shock when they forget to be humble. They will find that experiencing a single speed bump leads to people leaving their side. They may also suddenly find that the same friends are now flocking around the next successful person.

---

[1]https://www.hindustantimes.com/india/why-me-god/story-W8iubhxJ2caFUrH7C9nXDN.html

One is forgotten like the flavor of the month bygone. I remember the famous story of a superstar movie actor from Bollywood. He was extremely successful and was considered the finest actor by all during his heyday.

Just like Icarus, this distorted his worldview. He was convinced that there could never be anyone better than him. His self-importance only inflated further with the gathering of flatterers and fair-weather friends around him.

He used to meet his followers every evening, and the scene would be like a *darbar*, with him as the Sultan. He was intoxicated by all that flattery and attention. People around him praised him with eloquent words: words they did not actually believe. They only whispered to him the things he wanted to hear. However, they were not truthful words. Why did they do this? The actor had a habit of rewarding the person who praised him the best. He had incentivized his positive feedback.

So even the self-affirmations he gleaned from his daily interactions with people were derived from false praise. People were not being genuine. But he was so far gone in the intoxication of his hubris that he started believing such claims.

He started behaving like a star who was not being paid his due by the filmmakers. He started to get the reputation of being difficult. Moreover, new talent was always coming into the industry. Filmmakers now had a choice when it came to casting their actors. They preferred actors who gave more importance to their craft than to their pride. Soon, people started leaving his *darbar*. The superstar had finally come crashing down. He then realized that his adoring audience were opportunists and did not genuinely think as highly of him as they had previously described.

In contrast, I would like to give you the example of another megastar. In recent times, this actor had featured in a string of films that failed at the box office. But he remained humble and worked harder than ever to reverse the trend. His attitude and endeavor only endeared him to the industry.

He approached his roles as an actor and not as a star. It was this sincerity and humility that saw directors and producers approaching him with new projects. They strongly believed that he could make a comeback. He had built up so much credibility and standing within the industry that filmmakers would rather cast him than the bonafide star. These are just two examples.

If you look around, you are sure to find innumerable examples of people who let their fame get to their heads and allowed it to influence their attitude and behavior. There is a reason many childhood tales exemplify the moral that pride goes before a fall.

I can understand that getting praise is a powerful way to boost your self-worth. But do not allow it to inflate your importance. The example of my father's life played a crucial role in how I have lived my life. I make sure to keep my feet planted firmly on the ground. I ensure that I always remember my roots.

It does not matter what position I hold in my life; I always will help people no matter their station in life.

## Humility in Our Relationships

One of the tenets that I live by is that all are equal, and I behave the same way with everyone. I saw how my father interacted with the powerful political figures and the household help. His mannerisms and interactions never varied. I, influenced by my observations of him, also practice the same. It is a mantra that I repeat to myself.

I must remain grounded. I must be a down-to-earth professional. I may reach a sought-after position or be accorded a prestigious role. But I should not compromise on this trait. There is no scale to measure my human interactions and relationships.

I have heard of people who evaluate their relationships based on the benefits that can be accrued. However, my father showed me that our lives should instead be based on how we can serve humanity. So, even today, I cherish and religiously follow my father's practice of not discriminating against people and behaving according to the status they hold in their lives.

I have no qualms in hugging the seemingly simple security guard or pantry boy. They contribute in their own way to the development of an organization and its success. I do not even entertain a second thought when it comes to shaking their hands and initiating a conversation with them. I have done so for many years. They may not have the titles you wish to associate with, but they are people who also remind me of the important things in life. In fact, I have even saved their contact numbers on my mobile phone. I converse with them regularly and even forward them jokes that I find funny. They reciprocate in the same manner.

Some people may wonder how I am able to cultivate such an attitude toward everyone. My father made me understand that we all have this capacity within us. You do not need someone to tell you that you ought to be affectionate and respectful toward everyone. We have the human qualities of sympathy and empathy. However, our worldview gets distorted as we grow up. We get bogged down by societal and peer pressures. We are dictated by the image we want to present to the world. This is where humility helps to temper those distractions. Humility will remind you to do the right thing.

It will help you cut through the pressure lines of appearances and images. So, this brings us to the important question. How do we develop humility? Humility is one of the hardest traits to develop because it requires understanding and acceptance of yourself. It plays an increasingly greater role as you ascend the heights of achievement and success. It is about understanding and accepting who you are as a person, and not basing this on your status. Do not think of humility as putting yourself down. It is instead displaying the highest amount of confidence, self-acceptance, and self-awareness.

It is quite easy to be humble when you are at the bottom of a building, say on the ground floor (e.g., in a new job or a junior position). As you climb the ladder to higher and senior roles, you will attract more people around you.

Some of them may make you believe that you are akin to a God in their eyes. They will be ready with quick praises to flatter you and provide ready excuses for any minor setbacks. They will constantly say that you are the best, and their flattery may seduce you into believing that their words are the gospel truth. It is best to exercise utmost caution when listening to such people.

They are the people who have the potential to lead you astray and rob you of your humility. So, strive to be mature and listen to your innermost voice. That voice is your internal Godfather reminding you that pride can be as slippery as a banana peel. When you choose to ignore this inner voice and its warnings, you may end up becoming an arrogant and selfish leader who will likely slip on the proverbial banana peel and come crashing down harder and faster than your ascent had been.

You may hold the wrong assumption that one has to be loud and raucous to mark one's presence and to progress in the crowded commercial space. I would argue that your humility will instead provide you with far more and better opportunities to progress.

You must be aware that there is a strong reference check process in hiring practices today. If a company wants to hire you, they will not just look at you. They will also enquire about you. They may check with your colleagues and peers. They will not just look at your technical capabilities.

They will also look to see how good your interpersonal skills are. How do you behave with your peers? How do you treat your team members? These soft skills can make or break your career. Companies take this process seriously. They even hire a professional third party to get this research done on a potential candidate. They want a complete, unbiased view. Even CEOs, COOs, CFOs, etc., are checked on such references.

## To Cultivate Humility, Adopt One or More of the Following Practices:

### Practice Self-acceptance

An important element of humility is accepting yourself. We tend to obsess over our good, strong points or be depressed about our faults and weaknesses. We must not be stuck in denial or develop some form of inferiority complex. When you learn to accept your strengths and weaknesses, you will know where you need to learn more and where you can leverage to contribute.

This acceptance is the first step to improving positively. When you practice self-acceptance, you will also learn that nobody is perfect. When you come to this realization, you will not devalue others who may have some other shortcomings. This realization is ideal as you can then look to work on yourself and develop yourself better.

### Listen to Others

One of the most basic qualities of humility is giving equal value to others irrespective of their status. When you seek to listen to others, you are subliminally sending a message to the other party that you value them and their perspectives. It is an empowering gesture. When you spend time listening to others and understanding their feelings and values, you build trust; this enables people to express themselves and be comfortable around you.

When you are honest with them, you will be able to avoid the trappings of flattery. This trait is especially useful when you climb up the ladder as a leader. When you foster an environment that values listening, understanding, and accepting, people in larger teams will be comfortable coming up to you and sharing their thoughts and ideas.

It is essential that when you listen to others, you discard any pre-held notions or prejudices. It is important to remember that we do not always listen to solve people's problems. At times, they just need a space to vent their worries. Sometimes all they require is a patient ear. When you give them that space, you value them and respond to them as human beings.

**Practice Gratitude**

I am sure that you have come across an old phrase, *count your blessings*. This phrase has deep-rooted value in it. We may have enough to complain about in this world. But do not get stuck in a rut where you only find complaints around you. It would be best if you took the time to find peace and not get into a state of thanklessness. Be thankful for the breakfast you ate today. Be thankful for your job. Be thankful for your current salary that affords you the necessities of life. Be thankful for your family and friends who value you and your company.

Be thankful for the missteps and failings, for they have something to teach you. Humility comes from a place of positive outlook. If you are in a negative cycle, you end up wanting more or depreciating your self-worth. So, take time to stop, and just recall and remind yourself of everything that you are grateful for. If you start thinking like this, you will be thankful for everything that you have today, including your own life! Being grateful is a good way to cultivate a humbler and positive frame of mind.

**Take Help When Needed**

There is a misconception that if you ask for help, you project a sign of helplessness or weakness. This misconception comes from a misplaced sense of pride. We like to think that we are capable of solving our own problems. There are occasions when you know you need help, but your pride will hinder you from asking for assistance.

This scenario is especially hurtful when you have to ask for help from a junior or someone in a subordinate position. As I said earlier, your position does not define you. When you allow such thoughts to take control, you only stunt your own growth. Remember, humility is not assuming that you are wrong. It is about accepting that you are not infallible and opening your mind to the possibility of being wrong and asking for help. Humility will erase any feelings of shame or embarrassment.

**Mind the Language of Pride and Arrogance**

It is part of the human experience to feel good when you receive praise for doing something good!

There is nothing wrong with feeling good. It is a necessary boost to your own worth. However, do not let that feeling intoxicate you. When you keep indulging in that feeling, you will turn it into feelings of pride and arrogance. I am not saying that you should not accept compliments when you achieve something. Accept them, for you have put in the effort to achieve that accomplishment.

Feel that happiness, digest it, and move on. If you do not want to be smug, snobbish, or vain, learn to accept compliments with gratitude rather than pride. Feel thankful that someone has recognized your efforts. You can do so by simply reminding yourself that you are thankful for your ability. When you think in terms of pride in your skill, you tend to become arrogant. It is vital that you revisit the way you think. Think in positive terms of thankfulness and not in negative terms of pride. As the saying goes, what you think, you become.

**Ask for Feedback from Others Regularly**

This is an important habit to cultivate. It is a mixture of listening and minding your pride. When you ask for feedback from others, you open your circumstances to a more holistic and wider perspective. If you only look at things from your angle, there may be things that are missed. Let us say, for example, you enter a maze. Now you have two options to negotiate the maze. At crucial encounters, you could ask someone for clues or help. This particular someone would have a bird's eye view of the maze. The other option is to navigate it by yourself.

Which of the two options do you think is the better one? This habit is even more important for leaders. When you receive feedback, you will know if your conduct unintentionally rubs people the wrong way. We all can gain from hearing what others think about us.

Make a process and ask others to provide feedback, preferably anonymously, and insist on honest feedback from them. Some of the feedback may hurt you. But learn to take these in your stride and be grateful, and then make your list of self-improvements. An ideal feedback survey should take into account what you are doing right as well as what you are doing wrong. In other words, try to understand what actions of yours are considered good and what is it that rubs people the wrong way.

Find below a self-assessment worksheet that will help you understand where you may have let your pride and arrogance dictate your behavior. The worksheet will help you keep track of the habits you could inculcate from the list above.

| Find Your Godfather Inside You | Humility | Write Here |
|---|---|---|
| Learning Exercise *(Pride and Arrogance) | Recall examples of where you might have shouted at others or been rude to them. It could have been to a waiter in a restaurant or the attendant in the parking lot. It could also be the cashier at the grocery store payment kiosk or your subordinate in the office. | |
| | Examine your response. Grade yourself on a scale of 1 to 10: 1 being extremely rude and unnecessary and 10 being acceptable behavior. Put yourself in the other party's shoes and look at the situation. Would you have found it acceptable if you were at the end of such an action? | |

|  | Now imagine how you would like to respond to the same situation if given another chance, or how you should have ideally behaved. Try to attain 10/10 on self-score for Humility. |  |
|---|---|---|
|  | In your self-assessment, if you had scored anywhere less than 10, what habit would you like to practice to make it a 10? |  |
|  | Practice the decided habit every day. |  |
|  | Follow-up by practicing the habit thrice daily for ten days – morning, afternoon, night. |  |
|  | Subsequently, follow-up by practicing the habit twice daily for ten days – morning, night. |  |

|  | Then follow-up by practicing the habit once daily for ten days, at night. |  |

*The above learning exercise is for "pride and arrogance."

You may develop similar exercises for other traits of humility as explained under the section "To cultivate humility in self, think of one or more of the above practices."

# 3
# COURAGE
Overcoming fears and building the courage, and grace under pressure

> *"I learned that courage was not the absence of fear, but the triumph over it. The brave man is not he who does not feel afraid, but he who conquers that fear."* – Nelson Mandela

## Face Your Fears; Hiding from Them will Only Hinder and Hurt

One of the most significant lessons I learned about courage was during my early days as an Assistant Medical Superintendent. The year was 2005 and I was assigned to a big private hospital in New Delhi. As I was fresh into management, my days were spent learning from others. I spent a lot of time observing others. How did my seniors react to different emergencies? How did they handle the pressure? How did they communicate their messages? There was so much to learn.

It was during these days that a media report tainted the name of my hospital. A particular incident had occurred one evening at the hospital and the media reports had unleashed a torrent of negative publicity. The next morning all the media channels and journalists landed at our hospital. The news had been sensationalized, even as the hospital management was scrambling to get to the facts of the matter.

The complaint made by the patient's family got the maximum airing time on news channels, and newspapers too dedicated many column inches to this story.

In modern parlance, you could say that the story became viral. The immediate cost was that the hospital earned a bad reputation. However, we had to get to the bottom of the story. So, the entire hospital management team was summoned the next day. There were four Assistant Medical Superintendents, including me. We used to work on a shift basis that spanned 24 hours. But on this day, all of us were asked to be present. The four of us were directed to sit at the back of the proceedings.

As the matter was discussed, it came to light that one of my fellow Assistant Medical Superintendents was the only management personnel who was present during the incident. It happened late in the evening, and no other seniors were available as it was off-duty hours. When my colleague spoke haltingly, we realized that the hospital was not to blame for this incident. The patient's family had been unruly, aggressive, and unreasonable. They went to the media first and presented their version of the events.

When the matter was explored further, we found out that there was only one mistake on the hospital's part. Wanting to know the other side of the story, the journalists had come to the hospital to speak with my colleague. However, when he saw the cameras and recorders, he got scared. He did not want to face the media. He went into hiding and switched off his cell phone. He was not available to provide any clarifications to the media, and he had cut off all forms of communication. This also meant that he could not consult with his seniors for any guidance or advice either. He also could not inform the hospital management of the incident.

When the journalists could not reach the concerned colleague, they suspected that the patient's family's story could be true. This was when the hospital lost control of the incident and narrative. My colleague's silence and reluctance to face the media enabled the news channels to broadcast the story from a one-sided perspective. The hospital management made every effort on their part to sort out the issue. Much of the negativity the story caused could have been avoided if only my colleague had not gone into hiding.

This particular episode taught me that it is important that we face the situation however difficult it may be. Face the problem and do not run away from it.

Choosing to hide from a problem is akin to what the myth says about the ostrich. There is a popular myth that when an ostrich spots a predator or a hunter, it hides its head in the sand instead of fleeing the spot. The motto being out of sight, out of mind. While it is not true, it is a beautiful analogy for running away from trouble. The situation or crisis does not mitigate by itself.

You need to face it and resolve it. I firmly believe that you should approach any critical situation with honesty. Do not try to run away from it or try to dress it up differently. Take the responsibility. Even if it is a mistake of your own doing, it is always better to be upfront about it. If you choose to address it in any other way, you will make things far more complicated. It does not matter if it involves your personal or professional life. Face your problems head-on with honesty and accountability.

**Tests of Leadership**

If you want to be a leader, you have to learn to face challenging and tough situations. There is always something to learn from these situations. They will be the making of you. Cast your mind back to the first time you rode your bicycle unassisted. Did you shrivel up in fear? Did you give up cycling because it was scary to balance and not fall while pedaling simultaneously? You might have stopped immediately or stopped after a short ride; you may have perhaps even fallen. But you would have learned how to ride that bicycle by getting back on it again and riding it until you learned to balance properly. That muscle memory would then have helped you move on to riding other motorized two-wheelers. So, do not be overly worried about tough situations. Consider them as learning opportunities to improve yourself.

First, let us understand what courage is. Courage can be summed up simply as the innermost strength to take action or face the situation when a voice from within urges you to run away. It is the mental and moral strength you have to withstand fear, danger, difficulty, and tough situations. It is about having control over your fears to win. It is the ability to win over something that scares or frightens you. It is the ability and willingness to face pain, uncertainty, or intimidation. If you notice, it is not, as Mandela said, the absence of fear. It is about looking fear in the face and asking it to do its worst, for you will do your best.

The more tough situations you face, the more courageous you become. Courage does not come in an instant. It is a habit that you build over time. Think of how a diamond is made.

It is subjected to the greatest pressure before it comes out shining. So, think of your challenges in the same way. Think of how you can become a diamond. If you choose to ignore or run away from your troubles, you are only subconsciously creating an escapist mindset. Such a mindset will only see pitfalls even when opportunities present themselves.

Show me any disappointing professional career, and I will show you an escapist mindset. Show me a successful leader, and I will show you a courageous attitude. Remember, if you hide and escape from your troubles, they will come seeking you. Even if you think that the situation is resolved temporarily, it may flare-up in the future with even more severe consequences.

So, the next time you come across a tough situation, do not run. Face it and deal with it. You will grow from it and be better prepared for challenges the next time. Even if you falter, you will find that your confidence is boosted. You become tougher and more resilient. The result would be that you are sharper and better equipped to face even bigger challenges. These challenges will go a long way in making you an effective leader. They will help you consolidate your success and ensure that you sustain that success.

## Endurance in an Epidemic

On a personal note, COVID-19 has been a trying time for everyone. It has tested most people's mettle. I have seen many people face this adversity with courage. There has never been a greater test for humanity in the last 100 years. You may have seen the statistics and the news stories of the toll this virus has taken. But I saw great examples of courage daily.

While this has no scientific backing, I think that courage has been a crucial part of recovery. I have worked with my team in the wards with COVID-positive patients and ICUs. We always made sure to give our time and company to these patients and embolden them. We did not want them to feel alone.

We shared our company as well as courage with these patients. We used two covers of protection when visiting the COVID wards. One was in the tangible form of the PPE.

The second protection was the inner courage my team and I donned when we regularly did our rounds in the wards and ICUs. I was fortunate not to contract this disease. Perhaps I may have even contracted the virus, but my immune system powered by courage probably did not allow the virus to sustain within. As I said, this is not a scientifically backed claim.

It is more of an intuitive observation based on my experiences during those harrowing months. I saw patients who were initially scared and at the lowest levels of courage, become emboldened by our support and get rid of the disease after two weeks of severe difficulty. I can say that perhaps the exhibition of courage in a healthy individual (may not be the case where someone is carrying some other pre-existing conditions) enhances their inner immunity to uplift the immune response.

I must stress that this observation is based on personal experiences.

> *"Courage is the most important of all the virtues because, without courage, you can't practice any other virtue consistently. You can practice any virtue erratically, but nothing consistently without courage."* – Maya Angelou

I, too, built up my courage from facing situations such as the hospital defamation case that I mentioned earlier. I learned from confronting many tough situations in my early days as the Assistant Medical Superintendent. However, I think I had a great lesson in courage long before I became a professional.

## Grit in the Face of Grief

As I mentioned before, my father was a High Court judge. However, he unexpectedly met his demise when I was in the 12th grade. I was one of five children. Our elder sister had been married eight months before his passing away. However, none of us four boys had finished our education. I was in the 12th grade. My elder brother was pursuing his engineering degree. I had two kid brothers who were in the 9th and 7th grades.

I still remember the events of that day, August 3, 1989, as if it happened yesterday. I was in my classroom when some of my father's colleagues who were judges came to collect me from my school. I felt tense for some reason.

I was nervous, but I accompanied them anyway as they were taking me home. As we neared the government-allotted accommodation, I saw a startling sight. There were many people sitting silently.

I immediately recognized some of the senior lawyers and judges of the state among them. I had seen them previously on festive occasions when they came home to greet my father. But on that day, I could almost see the gloom that pervaded the air. I was feeling increasingly nervous, but nobody told me why I was brought home.

The previous day, my father, along with my mother and elder brother, had left for Delhi. A colleague of my father's then told me that someone was picking up my two younger brothers from their school as well. Then I was told that my father had summoned us to Delhi. I could sense that there was something they were hiding from me. I did not have any untoward thoughts as my family had been hale and healthy when they traveled to Delhi. We were informed that two senior judiciary members would accompany us on the flight trip to Delhi. The Chief Minister had personally conveyed that we were to be brought to Delhi safely.

This was the age when telecommunication was still in its infancy, and there were no cellphones available. So, I had no way to communicate with my family to find out what was happening. I was the elder of the three children, and I had a vague sense of foreboding even as my younger brothers were being naughty and having fun. They were still young and were not yet aware that the world could be a trying place. I probably knew by then that something bad was awaiting us in Delhi, but I did not want to think or guess what it could be.

When the flight landed in Delhi, we were received by one of my cousins and a few officers. We were then whisked to the State Guest House where I thought I would find my father, mother, and elder brother. Even as we were being driven there, I could sense a growing feeling of disquiet. But I stayed silent, trying to ward away all bad thoughts. When we reached our destination, I could see that none of my family was there. It was eerily quiet, and we met another senior colleague of my father's. I could see that he seemed a little down. However, he hugged all of us and told us that we needed to rush to Gwalior, our hometown. We were told time was of the essence, and we would be traveling by road immediately. On hearing this. I felt a sinking feeling in my stomach, and I was speechless.

It was already 9 pm, and a trip to Gwalior by road would mean crossing the precarious Chambal area brimming with dacoits. Nobody dared to travel by those roads at night.

However, the government sent us armed guards and vehicles to escort us safely to Gwalior and we reached at 2:30 am. My unease only increased as we neared our house. The lights were lit bright, but there seemed to be darkness in the air. Then I saw a hearse outside our door. My brothers and I entered the house, scared. It took me a second to recognize my father shrouded in a white cloth. A wreath sent by the Governor of the State was on him. My heart sank to the bottom of my stomach.

I remember everything that followed in vivid detail. I could not stop crying as I came to comprehend the situation. My younger brothers were beside me, crying as well. The grief we felt seemed inexhaustible. But our tears did come to an end at some point. Then my elder brother walked up to us. I could see that he, too, had cried for a long time. He then told us to go and meet our mother. When I heard that, I broke down afresh.

This time I was crying for my mother. I was scared to meet my mother. I could not fathom how broken she would be as she had lost her support in my father. She was a homemaker and had depended upon my father to run the household. I knew that the moment I saw her devastated, I would be broken further.

However, with tremendous reluctance, I went to meet my mother. When I saw her, all my preconceptions were completely blown away. I did not find a broken woman. I found a resolute one instead. She seemed like a bastion of strength. Even as we were still taking in the fact that we had lost our father, she projected courage and grace with her words. Her voice never wavered, and the warmth of her hug gave us tremendous solace. Her expressions gave us strength when we needed it the most. I will never forget the words she uttered next. "I will be your father, and I will be your mother. Your father has entrusted me with the responsibility to see that you grow up well and are cared for. I will ensure that to the best of my ability."

Those words have stayed with me all through these years. She was a picture of courage and willpower. My mother, until that fateful day, projected the image of a timid homemaker. But on that day, she transformed herself and proved to be the bulwark of the family in the toughest of times.

As I had mentioned earlier, my father had never exploited his position for any undue financial gains. Therefore, at the time of his passing, we did not have much savings.

So, my mother had to contend with the loss of her husband and the financial burdens, especially with four children yet to complete their education. But on that day, and ever since, she has never faltered. She was an oasis of comfort and her reassuring voice and expressions helped wither away our grief.

My father taught me honesty, integrity, and humility. My mother taught me courage. She, too, like my father, lived it as an example for me. She faced all adverse challenges head-on and never shied away or ran from them.

Each time we face adversities or adversaries in our life, they teach us to be stronger the next time. Our inner Godfather will always want us to face our problems head-on despite the fear they might incite in us. The inner Godfather knows that the more we handle issues, the stronger we become, and more likely to metamorphose into better leaders.

When I mention the two incidents from my life in this chapter, it is not with the intention that each of you should experience the same. I am referring to how you can develop your mindset to face the world.

There will always be a voice that may whisper that running away would be a far more comfortable option. When you run away, you are not sparing yourself. You are only permitting yourself to run away constantly. When you run away constantly, you will only regress. You need the pressure to grow and thrive.

Think of going to a gym. You need to subject your muscles to a lot of pressure over a protracted period of time to sculpt your body to the image you like. Similarly, you need the pressure borne out of tough situations to shape your mental and emotional make-up into a resilient and tough mindset.

Even as a tiny whisper speaks to your psyche tempting you to run, listen for another inner voice. This inner voice would be that of your inner Godfather. It will suggest that you find a way to show your resistance. It will ask you to face your fears head-on and find a solution. It is about tuning in to the right frequency. Listen to it. Build up your mental strength and develop mental toughness and watch yourself grow to tackle larger and bigger challenges.

## The Contagiousness of Courage

Face your challenges head-on. Do not tarry when you are thrown a curveball. Adapt to the situation and find yourself evolving. Every tough situation is an opportunity to learn and develop. They are practice sessions.

They will help you prepare for the bigger and stronger challenges you will face in your life. If you are a leader, an entrepreneur, or a professional, your professional success will be determined by the number of fears and challenges you faced rather than ducked. And when you keep fighting, you will find that courage is a contagious quality. People will be encouraged by your courage.

> *"Our deepest fear is not that we are inadequate. Our deepest fear is that we are powerful beyond measure. It is our light, not our darkness that most frightens us. We ask ourselves, 'Who am I to be brilliant, gorgeous, talented, fabulous?' Actually, who are you not to be? You are a child of God. Your playing small does not serve the world. There is nothing enlightened about shrinking so that other people won't feel insecure around you. We are all meant to shine, as children do. We were born to make manifest the glory of God that is within us. It's not just in some of us; it's in everyone. And as we let our own light shine, we unconsciously give other people permission to do the same. As we are liberated from our own fear, our presence automatically liberates others."* –
> Marianne Williamson

I can attest to the above from my personal experiences. Whenever I allowed fear to crop up, even in the form of a minor hesitancy, it has actually pushed me further back. So, I have always looked at developing my confidence to never back down from any challenging situation. This trait is especially critical for a leader.

One of the best stories that embodies the quote above is the story of Ken Carter, who was a high school basketball coach at Richmond High School. Carter was different from other high school coaches. He knew that most of his students came from impoverished conditions. These conditions would see students drop out of school and turn to crime.

Carter made his students sign contracts which demanded that they maintain certain academic and behavioral standards. He believed that they had to be excellent academically to excel outside the game and improve their impoverished conditions.

When the students failed to meet these requirements, he famously locked out his team from practice and playing. Even when the school, parents, and the community bayed at him, he did not wilt under the pressure. He faced them courageously with faith in his methods. His students responded and stood with him. Eventually, they all went on to college and found respectable jobs, and worked for the community.

What is the main duty of a leader? A leader must find solutions during times of crisis and lead his team through tough situations. Carter knew that if his wards had to live a better life, he had to take a stand and lead them to that better life.

But if you retreat from challenges, you will never be able to lead. Leaders are known for their courage, and people look up to them during dark times. Leaders are not born; they are made. They are made when they face tough situations which develop their problem-solving skills and hone their instincts and mental resilience.

So, how do we build up our courage? Start by doing something small. I am not asking you to find your courage to do something outlandish. There are many activities in our daily life that need courage. It could be as simple as asking a difficult question. Sometimes we may be worried about how our questions would be perceived by others. Will I come across as a fool if I ask this question? There is an old Chinese proverb that goes like this: He who asks a question is a fool for five minutes; he who does not ask a question remains a fool forever.

Take the courage to ask the question. Another action that can help build our confidence is confronting an adverse remark or act.

Sometimes we may not respond to an adverse situation as we do not want to escalate tensions or put a wrinkle in a relationship. But when you do so, you let resentment build in your heart. So, find the courage to sort out a situation instead of letting it fester. You could also find the courage to say 'no' when you want to say 'no.' Many people worry about the consequences of saying no. But you have to find the courage to say no. Here are some examples of actions that can build up your courage daily:

- Speaking up for yourself
- Speaking up for someone else
- Asking a difficult question
- Confronting an adverse act or remark

- Saying 'NO' when you mean 'NO'
- Creating a boundary line that someone might not like
- Speaking or accepting your truth
- Facing a conflict
- Showing your love
- Showing your anger
- Tolerating any type of pain
- Trying something new
- Challenging someone with a strong personality
- Feeling worthy of respect
- Believing that you are loveable

Courage builds confidence. In the darkest moments, when you are unsure and fearful of the outcome and your surroundings, courage can be the hand that warms you from the chill outside. When you are scared and find yourself frozen with doubt, it is courage that keeps you moving ahead to adopt either the fight or the flight strategy.

When you are afraid, you let your brain take a backseat. You let instinct drive you. Courage allows your brain back in the driving seat. It enables you to respond differently. If you want to be successful, you have to learn to overcome your fear.

It is even more essential when you are a leader. Cowardly leaders seldom lead. History is rife with examples of how such leaders lost their authority quickly.

When you are tasked with the responsibility of leading, you definitely need courage as you are now responsible not just for yourself, but for others too. There are people who will look to you to lead them out of the doldrums.

So, if you want to develop your courage, you should first confront your fears. Write them down. It could be anything like speaking in public, facing an enraged customer or client, asking questions, etc. There is nothing trivial about these fears.

Write them down so that you have a tangible feeling of what you fear the most. When you write them down, you will realize that the fear factor goes down a couple of notches as it is no longer an unknown factor. You know you will overcome it. I must remind you at this juncture that it is important for you to be candid and honest. Do not think that admitting your fears is a sign of weakness.

Once you pen down your fears, you can start with the following three-step practice.

Make a list of situations/things that scare you. It could also be scenarios in which you struggle for confidence. It could be situations that make you uncomfortable. It could be situations that make you panic. It can be a physical, mental, emotional, or spiritual situation.

Prioritize your list of fears. Choose the first thing you want to overcome. I would recommend that you start with something small. Build your courage in increments.

Start small and start with small victories. You can build up the momentum to challenge your biggest fears on the backs of your many small wins. This will also make your process more sustainable as you are more liable to give up if you fail in the first hurdle of challenging your biggest fear. There is no need to start running immediately.

We can begin just as we did when we were babies, by crawling before trying to walk. We can ease our discomfort and subject ourselves to greater pressure gradually. If there are places or situations where you feel you need professional help, note it down as well.

As I mentioned earlier, start small and practice your baby steps in facing challenges or fears every day. Adopt the follow-up schedule as described in the table below.

Let me provide you with an example. Let us say that you find it challenging to speak for yourself. It could be for many reasons. Let us see each baby step that will be a part of this process.

**Fear: I cannot speak for myself.**
The baby steps for overcoming this can be as follows:
1. Be clear on what point you want to make.
2. Practice saying your point out loud in front of a mirror.
3. Once you have done this a few times, speak it out in front of someone close to you. Ask for their feedback once you have done so.
4. Start a self-talking and self-appreciation habit. (In this case, keep affirming to yourself, "I am capable of speaking my truth.")
5. Record your voice saying your truth, and listen for self-improvement.
6. Practice saying 'no'

7. Practice saying "let me think about this before I answer."

# Affirmations

 I am capable of **speaking** my truth

I am not afraid to say **no** to the things I'm not comfortable with

 I am capable of **achieving** things I have dreamt of

I am **courageous**

 I am doing **my best** everyday

| Find Your Godfather Inside You | Courage | Write Here |
|---|---|---|
| Learning Exercise | Fear One (Name of the fear) Describe your fear | Steps that you decide to practice to overcome the fear (you can include any special training you want to undertake to help you, besides day-to-day practice):<br>1.<br>2.<br>3.<br>4.<br>5.<br>6. |
| | Fear Two (Name of the fear) Describe your fear | Steps that you decide to practice to overcome the fear (you can include any special training you want to undertake to help you, besides day-to-day practice):<br>1.<br>2.<br>3.<br>4.<br>5.<br>6. |
| | Fear Three (Name of the fear) Describe your fear | Steps that you decide to practice to overcome the fear (you can include any special training you want to undertake to help you, besides day-to-day practice):<br>1.<br>2.<br>3.<br>4.<br>5.<br>6. |

|  | Fear Four (Name of the fear) Describe your fear | Steps that you decide to practice to overcome the fear (you can include any special training you want to undertake to help you, besides day-to-day practice):<br>1.<br>2.<br>3.<br>4.<br>5.<br>6. |
|---|---|---|
|  | Practice the decided steps every day, in the following manner |  |
|  | Follow-up check for practice thrice daily for 10 days – morning, afternoon, night |  |
|  | Follow-up check for practice twice daily for 10 days – morning and night |  |
|  | Follow-up check for practice once daily for 10 days – at night |  |

You can create an excel sheet on the above lines, and create a full follow-up plan for 30 days, based on the above table. You can create a sheet for each fear, so that the follow-up can be done easily.

Alternatively, use small diaries for your follow-up plans. You can have one diary with over 120 pages, and create a follow-up plan for each fear, spread over 30 pages.

# 4
# DILIGENCE & DETERMINATION
## Decide. Commit. Succeed

*"What we hope ever to do with ease, we must first learn to do with diligence."*
– Samuel Johnson

**The Tree and the Fruit; My Father and I**

When I was selected as one of the top 10 healthcare leaders of 2020–2021, I could not help but visit my past like I have been doing for every success that I have achieved. I go into the flashback mode in my alone times, reflecting on the bittersweet memories of what led me to this point in life.

A point where I am able to call myself successful. So, when I closed my eyes and thought about how my life had been over all these years, I realized that some basics of life have played such an important role. Many things that went unnoticed at one time, things that I did not pay any attention to at all, are making sense now all of a sudden. I realize their value and contribution now.

It is natural as a human, to look back and wonder how different things would have been had you acknowledged the things you have now realized the value of.

However, it is not in one's hands to change the way things have panned out; in fact, there must be some truth to the saying that everything happens for your own good. As I have mentioned, the path of reminiscence is mostly bittersweet.

Therefore, when I received this recognition, I sat on the sofa in my living room, closed my eyes, and went back to my childhood. Back to when I was 10 or 11 years old, a rebellious child with no care in the world and no clue of the person I would eventually become. As always, flashbacks take me straight to my father. Before I can think of anything or anyone else, I remember my father: a serious, quiet, and extremely hardworking professional. He was a highly principled man, honest to his core, a practicing lawyer who would never go to court even for the least important case without thorough and complete diligence. Even if there came a situation where he had to abandon everything, he would not give up his work and family. At that time, these things did not make much of an impression on me and I could not relate to them, being a young brat in the 4th standard, who was ready to hit or break everything he could lay his hands on or fight with anyone to any extent.

Those days, my evenings were spent playing cricket with my elder brother, and we would not come home until it became pitch dark; sometimes, we had to be literally pulled inside the house! My father was completely contradictory to who I was back then; he was a calm person, and I have never heard him shouting at anyone. Even though it was not a bizarre concept, at that age, you do not quite understand the essence of being calm and collected. Focused and full of principles—these qualities in my father never stood out to me that much at that time.

Although I was not able to connect with my father's virtues, I now realize that somewhere, somehow, I had been absorbing those same qualities of my father. Silently soaking up his values like a sponge, I learned how being diligent makes a difference in a person's success. My father was renowned for winning most of his cases, almost cent percent, owing to the high diligence with which he prepared for every single case he would pick up. Be it a small one or a big one, his diligent preparation would be equal for all the cases. It was generally believed that a lawyer would go to any extreme to win the case for his clients, but despite being a lawyer, my father lived a life of principles.

Sometimes even the best of people choose the easier path in life, especially when the path that is easy and the path that is right appear extremely identical. But not so in my father's case; he always put his integrity first. I think he understood how important it was, to be honest with oneself.

He would choose a case only if there was no need for twisting the facts around and if and only if it was not going to be harmful to anybody. Perhaps the reason why he was elevated to be a Judge of the High Court was on the basis of his clean image, and the diligence and principles on which he stood firm all through his life.

However, even after becoming a Judge of the High Court, he understood the enormity of his role in the lives of people whose cases he would preside over and pass his judgment on. His preparation for the cases he was presiding over never went down. He would burn the midnight oil for every case he was called to judge, irrespective of whether it was a small one or a big one.

I believe I was subconsciously absorbing these values and that is the reason I remember all this, despite being a rebellious kid. The values and principles I saw in my father shaped my personality as well. As children, you mirror your parents. I mirrored my dad's best traits, not knowing that my personality would grow to be similar to his professional personality. And I really would not have it any other way. It has taught me so much I never realized I needed.

I was fortunate to have my father as a role model in these aspects. However, this may not be the case for many people. Sometimes, people do have role models in their lives, but they do not realize it the way I never realized it until I grew up and tasted success. I had to trace my way back to understand what brought me here. But the undisputed fact is that these virtues are so much more required when you do not have a Godfather to hold your finger and guide you through your career, as you enter the professional world, especially if you want to be a successful leader. If you do not have a role model, it is up to you then to become one for yourself.

## Diligence and Success

Diligence is one of the basic needs for success, in all spheres of life. Success attained with the sheer power of diligence, is a long-term success, a sustainable success, and a valuable success. Since it is achieved after long hours of work, homework, persistence, and suffering, it is most likely to formulate diligence. Whether you are a student, an employee, or an employer, if you practice diligence, you are guaranteeing yourself success in whatever you undertake. Diligence makes you an asset to your organization and leads you toward the leadership role and your definition of success, eventually.

Let us talk about success. Everybody, all of us, all of you, want to be successful. The longing for success is natural; in fact, it is necessary. This longing and dreaming about success are the first steps required to be taken toward the path of success. However, success is never accidental; it never comes only by dreaming or longing for it. It does not arrive overnight. The definition of success defers from person to person, but the road to success remains the same.

It needs tremendous diligence, tremendous persistence, and dedication. This habit of being diligent and working hard to attain the desired result is a very painful activity coupled with even sacrifices. Hence, this chapter is aimed at helping you to achieve your goals which you believe will make you successful, so that you go beyond just longing and dreaming of success and work on converting your longings and dreams into reality all by yourself. You will be able to identify every single quality any leader who is a human being (obviously) can ever think of or has ever gained, right inside you, without searching for a Godfather in the outside world.

Therefore, irrespective of your field of knowledge, interest, activity, or profession, if you make a persistent effort with hard work toward your goal, you will eventually be successful in accomplishing them. Your efforts will not be futile anymore. This constant habit of persisting with hard work to achieve your goals is the diligence which every individual has to master, to be a successful leader.

There was a hardworking man, a laborer. He had a wife whom he loved very much She happened to sustain some severe injuries and was in a critical state. They were from a secluded village, and his wife needed proper medical care which was available only in the nearest city. The man was determined to get his wife to safety, but it was not so easy. There was a big mountain between their village and the city which needed to be crossed, and it was not an easy task at all. His wife's condition was beginning to worsen. This was an emergency, and the only way he could reach the city was to climb the mountain carrying his wife. He had no doubt in his mind that he would do the impossible task of crossing the mountain that stood between their village and the city. But, as fate would have it, his wife expired before he could take her there. He was devastated and angry. But he had also discovered a new purpose in his rage. The man was so shaken by his wife's loss, that he decided to carve a path through that mountain.

People in his village made fun of him and no one would help him. He began working all by himself. Despite numerous hurdles, he continued working on his goal, progressing a little each day. Finally, in about 22 years, he was successful in carving a tunnel through the mountain, which connected his village to the nearest city.

Even though this story sounds unbelievable, this is not fiction. This is the true story of Dashrath Manjhi, the laborer, whose wife died under the abovementioned circumstances in 1959.

He went on to dig a tunnel through the mountain, all by himself, taking 22 long years. What kept him going were his diligence, persistence, and determination. There cannot be a true-life example more authentic and stronger than this for what diligence and determination can do for a person's success.

William Penn once said, *"Patience and diligence, like faith, remove mountains."* In Dashrath's case, it did so literally. Diligence is a vital trait for any human being, whether he/she is in a professional workspace or not. Whether you are craving for career development or looking to become successful, you need to be 100 percent committed, and to stay committed, you ought to be diligent. It is not an easy path. It takes hundreds of self-reminders to focus and jump back on the track and keep pushing yourself.

**Wicket-taking Timber**

To this end, you need to work first and foremost on identifying your virtues which come under diligence and determination. You will find to your surprise that you already possess these qualities and are exhibiting these in your day-to-day life. Once you are done identifying your qualities, it is just a matter of consolidating them for the better: to use them for bigger causes and to create and write your own success story. Let me give you another example.

When I was in the 10th grade, I had to change my school. In my new school, an inter-class cricket match was being organized. This was a new school, and I did not know anyone yet. But, being a passionate cricketer in my childhood, like most of us, I pleaded to be included in my class team. Surprisingly, I managed to enter the team as a bowler.

However, our class captain, Himanshu, who happened to be a state-level player in the under-16 category, did not give a single over for me to bowl.

Our team was failing badly, and two of the middle-order batsmen from the opposing team were having a great day. We just could not take them out and we were slowly inching toward losing the match (we had batted first, and I had not got a chance to bat). At this point, I once again started pleading with my captain to give me an over to bowl. He totally ignored my pleas, but I was determined to have it. So, I kept pestering him after every four or six that was hit by the opposing team. Finally, I succeeded, and my time arrived. The captain gave me an over to bowl. I knew that this would be my first and last over if I did not perform well. I knew I would not be given another chance, and therefore, was under a lot of pressure. But I decided to put my everything into it.

I could not believe my luck with what happened next. I cleaned up both the batsmen in the same over. The team was overjoyed. I had scored myself another over to bowl, the second last over of the match. It was all up to me now to take my team to the finish line. And to my luck the cricket gods smiled down on me that day; I could not believe it when I took another three wickets in the next over! In just two overs, I had taken five wickets, and our class team actually won the match! What I did not know was that the school team was also being selected based on the performance in these matches. I found out the next day that my name had been included in the school team to represent our school in an inter-school tournament that was going to take place the next week.

This time, I was given the very first over to bowl, probably based on my previous performance in the inter-class match. I used to be a pacer. I was over the moon when once again, the opposition team was all over the place, and I ended up taking six wickets in four overs (the quota per bowler). Later on, to contribute evenly, our batsmen scored 56 runs to win in just 12 overs, and we won the match! We had done it.

For certain reasons, I could not participate in the rest of the tournament. But my classmate, Himanshu, who was already playing for the State in the under-16 team, became a dear friend to me. He pointed out that I had sheer pace and he had not seen anyone bowling as fast as me in his playing teams. He insisted that I should attend the camp being organized for the selection of the team for that year's (1986–87) Vijay Merchant Trophy (under 16). He informed me that a cricket coach appointed by the State would be training all those who attended the camp.

Moreover, only those who had attended the training camp could participate in the trial to be held the next month, and the same coach was to be one of the selectors. I was not sure about it, but I decided to go ahead and join the camp. The training would start every day at 4 pm and go on until sunset. Our coach, Tickoo Sir, hardly paid any attention to me and my doubts grew about the usefulness of the camp. He was always busy with his regular students, training and coaching them to the extreme, and did not pay much attention to the numerous boys who used to come and go. His favorite player was Surjeet, who was a pacer like me. So, I used to watch keenly and learn as much as I could from afar. Though I was feeling ignored and left out by Tickoo Sir, I tried to gather whatever I could from all that was being taught to Surjeet.

After a week of ignorance, I decided to coach my own self. After returning home from school by 1 pm, I would ride my bike to the stadium. And I would practice under the scorching sun, alone in the entire stadium. I used to buy my own leather ball, and take it with me to the stadium. Three stones placed in the nets served as the wickets, as I used to practice my bowling. I tried to remember and put into practice whatever Tickoo Sir had been teaching Surjeet. There was an advantage to playing at the nets as the ball never went anywhere else, but would just get stuck there. After every bowling, I would walk up to the net behind the wickets space, pick up the ball, walk down to the run-up, and bowl again. I would repeat the same many times. It used to be terribly tiring in that heat, but I was clear what I wanted to do.

After about two weeks of my 'self-coaching sessions,' one day during my time of practice, just as I was walking back to my run-up after having picked the ball, I heard a loud stern voice say, "Who are you?" I looked back, a little shaken. It was Tickoo Sir. I was right. He had obviously never noticed me during the camp times! I stood in front of him, my head bent, and told him who I was and why I was practicing on my own. I told him that I was trying to do "self-coaching" based on whatever I had grasped when he taught Surjeet. He was speechless for a while. Then he came closer to me, took the ball from my hand, and poured out all about the basics of ball grip, seam, shine, run-up, and whatnot. It was as if he opened the entire book of fast bowling that day to me! He made me bowl a few balls in front of him, and from that day onwards, I became his best pupil, and all his focus shifted largely to me!

So much so, that he started half an hour early to coach me alone before the official time of the camp! I was thrilled that I could finally learn the way I desired to learn. The effort that was put in from both our ends eventually did lead to a lot of success. I am happy to state that I did get selected and went on to progress in cricket, playing at the Nationals, much ahead of my age!

We only realize who we were then when we look back. Today, when I look back at the entire episode, I clearly see I had exhibited considerable persuasion, a never-say-die spirit, an intense hunger to achieve something, untiring hard work, attention to homework, and, in totality, a great deal of diligence in my childhood. I never knew then that it was my inner Godfather who was teaching me these basics of leadership.

In my childhood, I never recognized it as actual diligence. I was too immature to derive any meaning out of anything at that time. But now when I look back, I know what it was that helped me succeed, and how important it still is, to practice and exhibit diligence on the road to success. Often, we are not aware of the outstanding qualities we possess. Sometimes, with time and limited use of those qualities, it might get blemished, or even lost. It is important, therefore, to take time to reflect on yourself, and analyze what your best qualities are, and put them to use. Polish them and implement them in your life, so that even without a guiding hand, you are able to navigate through any phase right into success.

I wanted to convey and emphasize these stories because there are a lot of takeaways here. Let us analyze some from the start.

1. I showed persistence when I insisted that I be included in the class team. I asked for a chance to bowl and did not give up until I had scored that chance.
2. I utilized the chance to the fullest. I exhibited hard work and determination when I put in my everything to do the best possible in my first over, which I thought would be my last over if not done well.
3. I continued my good performance; I got selected to the school team.
4. When I realized that I was not getting the coaching I wanted, I started doing my own coaching, and eventually, I was able to gain what I wanted. Hard work and homework are the pillars of success.

5. I was raw before the coaching. But after being coached, I turned into a much better cricketer and a winner. It means even if you have the raw talent, you must acquire technical expertise on the basic level to succeed.

When you take time to identify all the signs of diligence that you have showcased on a day-to-day basis, you will be able to bring back those qualities and polish them as you are already in possession of those virtues. You have to learn to be persistent with them, to practice them, and to excel in them even more. Identifying the signs of diligence that you already have and continuing with them is what is going to give you the confidence and an edge over everything you do. You will find success at your feet.

## The Need for Determination

Diligence tastes best when it is served with determination. Even though we would have heard these words very often, sometimes we forget what they mean and how important they are to lead a successful life. When we talk about determination, you cannot find a more fitting quote to remember than the one by Benjamin Franklin. He says, *"He that can have patience can have what he will."* To understand the word determination, you can take references from the previous story. The reason why I was able to bowl so well in my first over was that I understood I would not get a second chance and I had to be impressive at the first shot. I had to. I was determined, and so, I did it. I have mentioned earlier that, dreaming about a goal and longing for it is already the first step. Determination is more often than not derived from a dream. It is the positive surge of attitude to keep going no matter what, until you have achieved what you had aimed for. Determination is important.

I am reminded of another quote here. This one is by Ralph Waldo Emerson, and he says, *"Once you make a decision, the universe conspires to make it happen"*. It is true; if you are determined, many situations shift in your favor. When you give your best, the rest usually works out. Determination is not just about the luck of achieving your goal; rather, it is the acknowledgment that things could go wrong, but even when they do, I am going to get as close to my goals as possible. With every obstacle I face, I will remind myself of why I started this journey.

This acknowledgment makes our efforts meaningful, and gives us the strength and the spark to cross the finish line. Let us talk about determination a little more.

The MBBS course is neither an easy nor a cheap course to undertake. Even if you choose to pursue it from a Government Medical College, the books and other study materials are not cheap. They are quite on the expensive side. The cost only increases as you inch toward your final MBBS professional exam. In my time, it used to be one and a half years of 'professional' and not a semester of six months. During my first few years in the MBBS course, some of the senior doctors, who were known to my father, were helpful to me by lending me their resources.

However, in the final professional, the subjects are vast and purely clinical. You have no option but to buy only the latest editions of the textbooks, since medical science makes rapid progress and the editions are updated accordingly. Hence, my expenses in the final professional year had increased quite high.

In addition to the cost of buying books, I had to bear my basic living costs as well. I had to keep all my essentials in check, which limited my pocket money. Everything was getting spent on the needed resources. There was no way I could have asked my mother as I was mindful of our financial condition. Also, I could not even imagine taking a loan from anyone else as it was against my principles. Hence, I was finding it very difficult to continue the course and was in a constant state of worry and over-thinking. Should I drop out of MBBS? Or, what else should I do? It was getting difficult. Doubts mess with your mind. The easy way out here would have been to drop out of the course and see what else I could do, but it was my determination that forced me to not be negative and find a solution.

I decided that I was going to find a way out of this situation. There had to be a way. I started brainstorming all the things that could be done and that is when an idea came to me. I decided to start private tuitions for school children. This was a good plan. It could be done without any investment of money, but I was going to be investing something much greater: my time. The idea took off; I would spend the daytime in the Medical College attending classes, and in the evenings, I would take tuitions. This worked wonderfully for me. It helped me with the small but necessary amount of money to continue my MBBS course.

Honestly, this was not easy. Final MBBS requires a lot of detailed studying and time, being the crux of the entire five-year course. While all my classmates used to get time to do their self-studies or group studies after the classes, I used to be out teaching school children so that I could earn enough to provide the basic necessities for myself.

This included my books and transport costs among others. There were times when I felt demotivated. Following this kind of exhausting lifestyle right from your student days can easily lead to a burnout.

However, I would constantly remind myself that this was my own decision, and that it was giving me the requisite small income to continue my MBBS course, which I might have had to drop out of otherwise.

I needed to remind myself to look at the larger picture. These reminders would bring me back to my senses and leave me feeling rather more determined and happier about the entire matter. All the pain and all the tiredness would be worth the result I was looking at. I had to keep going. And I did just that.

The tough times in your life only make you more determined to get closer to your goal, and that determination is exactly what transformed me into the person I am today.

The challenges that I faced in those early days of my life were preparing me for the future, and I realize now how strong they actually made me to face the life ahead. There are a lot of learnings I would like to acknowledge from the challenges of my past:

1. Determination allows and motivates you to find a solution.
2. With determination, you can continue to walk on the path that you choose as your solution.
3. Determination brings you back to your purpose if/when you deviate away from it.

These learnings have been with me to date. I believe these learnings came from within me, from my own Godfather, and they have been handy, day in and day out, until today. The successful denouement of any challenge or any task demands diligence and determination. Any task that seems impossible may be achieved with enough diligence and determination. When you keep going, success is sure to come sooner or later, but without a doubt.

A diligent person is someone who exhibits persistence and hard work. He is the one who puts in an equal effort, whether it is doing something small or big. Being diligent is one of the most important attributes of a successful leader and even more so of an individual.

Here are a few steps which can help you to develop and practice diligence and determination in a more structured manner, for a glorious success story:

## Identify What Goal You Want to Achieve, However Small or Big:

This is called clarity of vision, and it not only gives you the direction to follow the goal, but will also make you passionate enough toward your goal to ensure that no type of discouragement can deviate you from your vision. As humans, it is inevitable that we might get distracted at times, but if you want to be successful, it is important to keep your eyes on the goal no matter how many times you lose track. If you miss out on the vision, it means you stand to lose the passion, direction, motivation, and enthusiasm to pursue your goals. Clarity of vision makes you stay focused even when it appears tough. It helps you to remain diligent, and diligence, in turn, transforms your dream into reality.

## Advance Planning Works.

Be it in our professional or personal lives, we want to achieve many things, and that is absolutely normal. However, in the absence of proper planning, we tire out, and many times, we fail to convert most of our goals into reality; we then have regrets in the latter part of our lives. Hence, once you have clarity of vision, plan in advance to pursue your vision in a stepwise manner. This will save you a lot of valuable time. However, planning in advance does not mean that you have to plan every detail from the start to the finish; it just means you should know which direction you are heading into. Even if you have a bit of trouble navigating through this step in the beginning, keep trying. We learn what works best for us by trial and error. The best way to plan early is to plan a day in advance. It is ideal to make plans for the next day only after completing the tasks for today. Bombarding yourself with too many tasks will only cause chaos and result in a mess.

Instead, finish what you have in hand and proceed sequentially.

**Excuses – Get Rid of Those.**

You have identified your vision, prioritized the things that need to be done, and started to plan in advance; but, when you take stock of the progress in your plans, you will realize that some of the steps are not going as per plan. You probably ask yourself, 'why?' and you come out with some reasons to defend yourself. The 'reasons' you identify should not just be excuses to defend yourself. It is your responsibility to get rid of these excuses and follow your plans with diligence to lead a successful life. Some reasons may be completely genuine and non-negotiable. But there are also some reasons that you give yourself only to procrastinate. Procrastination will not help you very much; so, it is vital to stay in touch with yourself and keep yourself in check to make sure you do not fall prey to excuses.

We all have that innermost voice that guides us in everything we do. Often it gives us positive suggestions; however, sometimes it can be a negative or fearful voice. If we begin to overthink a situation, we tend to spot every single thing that may go wrong and limit ourselves. Hence, the requirement is to listen to this innermost voice, our inner Godfather or intuition, that gives a positive suggestion. Make a habit of listening to it.

Over a period of time, you will see that fear has started to take a backseat. Only the positive voices are heard; this is what we mean when we say that someone gives us positive vibes! You need to inculcate the habit of listening to your inner voice; this will definitely help you in your march toward success. The most important traits of diligence and determination need to be developed and practiced as well.

Allow your personality or your character to soak up these values and make them your own. That is how you will become a positive person and go on to write your chapter of success.

However, this may be easier said than done for many; therefore, the journey toward this has to be worked on. As explained earlier, the first step is to identify and pen down what goal you want to achieve, or the vision you carry with you. If you are ambitious, if you are a dreamer, you have crossed the first step already. Once this is done, then the following steps are quite helpful and practically doable by all.

1. **Keep a planner:** This can be as simple as a pocket-size diary, or alternatively, keep one in your mobile phone itself. The purpose of having a planner is to have it handy with you so that you can keep checking it, whenever you want, wherever you are. This is to organize your day and maintain diligence and regularity.

   For example, you may be preparing for your exams or there may be due dates to keep note of for a semester, or there may be a competition or an interview and you have to cover a few topics or subjects; in such situations, a planner helps you assign time for each of your activities. Prioritize according to what you need to do first and prepare accordingly. This way, you will be more confident on that particular day as you know you are well prepared and ready to go. You will also not miss out on anything and invite unnecessary anxiety.

2. **Avoid clutter:** Do not include too many things in the planner. Do not get involved in too many courses and extra-curricular activities at a time, because it will then divide your focus and diminish the quality of your efforts. If you are a student, keep track of the drop/add periods schedule of your institute to make sure you can drop a class if needed. Cluttering will only make you feel overwhelmed, which in turn will disturb your mental peace and not let you complete the things you wanted to. Again, if you want to be successful, you have to learn to prioritize the tasks you have at hand based on the urgency with which they have to be completed.

3. **Plan an early start on your assignments, projects, or steps:** Waiting until the end to prepare for a big project, interview, exam, or speech will only make you more stressed than you have to be. Instead, making an early start will take a load off when the final time comes to deliver. When you procrastinate, you also tend to clutter. When you clutter up your schedule or life, you are causing your own downfall. Therefore, ensure that you check off the things on your planner as and when it is scheduled.

4. **Be flexible:** Sometimes, you may have to reschedule, rework, and re-evaluate your goals, for an unavoidable reason. Remember, THIS IS OKAY and a normal part of normal progress. The most important thing is being true to yourself. Do not confuse real reasons such as a sudden illness or a tragedy or the loss of a job with lame excuses. These are not excuses but are situations that you have no control over. Rather than mourning over the loss of time, you have to think like a leader: what do I do to make up for this? Some examples of excuses would be you want to hang out with your friends when you have a timeline or watch a movie to procrastinate and such.

5. **Get rid of distractions:** Spending too much time on anything which is stopping you from working on your action plans or steps is a distraction. It may be the internet, your phone, or the television, or even, just gossiping with your friends or colleagues. The best way to discipline yourself is by analyzing if the activity was helpful to you or not; use your pocket diary to do this by writing down the activity (E.g.: gossiped with a colleague) and categorize it as follows: time taken (E.g., 30 minutes), helpful or not helpful. This will serve as a reminder to you and stop you the next time you indulge in a similar activity. In this way, you can minimize or totally get rid of the distractions. You will see what a change this brings in your life as a professional.

6. **Break larger tasks into smaller steps:** This helps you be aware of the overall time needed for a task to get completed. Also, it allows you to schedule time for each task or subtask accordingly. For example, let us assume you have to deliver a speech or appear for an interview. This can be broken into these smaller steps:
Step 1: Understanding the headline of the topic or subjects to be covered.
Step 2: Arranging the material or knowledge base to prepare for these.
Step 3: Making a presentation or speech script or fine notes for the respective task. *(Tip: Keep the list of subheads to three items ideally—not more, not less)*

This way you will be able to stay focused. When you break down your tasks, it does not seem too much and you will be motivated just the right amount to complete it.

7. **Focus your energy on your goal**: Reminding yourself of your goals and why you are focusing on the task at hand, always helps. Moreover, self-talk does wonders; for example, once you have completed a step decided in the given time, tell yourself, "Well done" or "Thank you." Reprimand yourself if you have not done a task as per the plan! Reward yourself when you do something good. Remind yourself when things do not go as planned. This will help you keep your eyes on the road.

8. **Find an accountability group or a partner or a friend**: Identify someone who knows you well enough and share about your tasks and subtasks with them; they will be helpful in motivating you to make progress on your goals. (Sometimes, all you need is someone who is working on the same goals as you; for example, if you are trying to lose weight, you might try a weight-loss group or a friend or family member who is trying the same).
A lot of us perform really well when we are in a group as we can always receive feedback and tips, and even give some of our own away. However, keep in mind that you should not rely on your accountability group or friend completely, but only respect them in terms of encouragement and moral support.

Having understood the need for developing diligence and determination as part of your personality to achieve success and the basic concepts involved, and also having learned how you can go about it, it is time now to take the next step to actually go about it, in reality!

The following table will help you develop diligence and determination. You can create as many tables as you want to or as long a one as required. Once you fill up these columns, you will be mentally prepared for launching yourself!

| Find Your Own Godfather Inside You | Diligence & Determination | Write Here |
|---|---|---|
| Learning Exercise | Write down a difficult task that you have not been able to start despite wanting to, or have started but not completed. E.g., beginning an exercise schedule or wanting to lose weight, or wanting to do a part-time, correspondence, or off-campus learning course, or wanting to do a personality enhancement course, or wanting to complete a long-pending assignment, etc. | Steps decided to follow for completing this task in your day-to-day living: 1. 2. 3. |
| | Practice the decided steps every day, in the following manner | |
| | Follow-up check for practice thrice every day for 10 days – morning, afternoon, and night | |

| | Follow-up check for practice twice every day for 10 days – morning and night | |
|---|---|---|
| | Follow-up check for practice once every day for 10 days, at night | |

*Fill up the above and start bang on, and you will be a victorious leader soon! And a word of caution while preparing, do not try to do all of it at once in the early stages. Make regular short work plans over a specific time period and try to find some way to ignite a natural curiosity about the task; this will keep you motivated to reach the finish line, your goal, your task.

# 5
## DISCIPLINE
## A choice between pain of discipline or pain of regret and failure

*"It is ordained in the eternal constitution of things, that men of intemperate minds cannot be free. Their passions forge their fetters."* – Edmund Burke

**License and Punishment**

According to the dictionary, discipline is "the practice of training people to obey rules or a code of behavior, using punishment to correct disobedience." I would like to share some incidents from my life to help you understand what discipline is and how to attain it. Whenever I think about discipline or an orderly life, I recall my father.

He was a man of principle and regulation. He always valued discipline highly, and gave great importance to it in his life and in his children's lives.

The following is a real-life experience, and it is through this episode that I learned to be 'disciplined' in every situation from my father. This incident happened during my teenage days when my elder brother started riding a bike.

While handing him the bike keys, our father gave him a clear mandate to be followed. He instructed that the rules of riding a bike should never be compromised, irrespective of the situation.

He essentially stressed two aspects of bike riding: wearing a helmet and never going for triple riding (of course, he gave clear instructions on other factors as well).

I wondered why he stressed those two aspects! Having a probing and curious nature as a teenager, I was serious about following my father's mandates only in his presence! Whenever my brother and I left home on the bike, we wore our helmets following his directive; once we hit the road, the helmet was off the head and hanging on the side! We used to be extremely careful while returning home; we stopped our bike at a little distance from our house and swiftly donned our helmets before and then rode through the entrance to ensure our father saw us. In this way, we tricked him into believing that we always wore a helmet while riding the bike and made him have a good impression of us for following the traffic rules. We made use of the same ploy with regard to triple-riding, but my elder brother was caught by the traffic inspector one day, who confiscated his license.

He asked my brother to appear in the court of the traffic magistrate and pay the fine to get it back. When my brother went to court, the magistrate immediately recognized him as the son of our father (in the High Court hierarchy, our father occupied a superior position). The magistrate not only returned the license but also offered him a cold drink! After this incident, my brother did not have any qualms about violating the traffic rules as he lost all fear of being punished and he continued with his experiments! However, a few days later, the traffic police caught him again, seized his license, and ordered him to visit the traffic magistrate again.

The due date to appear before the magistrate was two days later, and till then, all these 'crimes' had to be hidden from our father. We were aware that he would be seriously displeased by our actions. Contrary to my brother's expectations of dealing with the situation like the previous time, the same day, the very same traffic magistrate, who had earlier given a cold drink to my brother, came to our home for some court-related work. He brought my brother's license along with him and handed it over to him in front of our father. My father was shocked on seeing this and my brother was caught red-handed!

He began rebuking my brother when he realized that this was not his first offense. He gave instructions to the magistrate that any further traffic violation cases involving my brother should be sent to the High Court, where he was the presiding judge.

My father warned my brother and told him that as the judge of the High Court, he would immediately suspend or cancel his driving license, and make sure that he does not commit such a mistake again.

All these gave me a rebellious feeling; I did not approve of my father's reaction to the incident. I questioned his anger toward us and his rude responses toward my brother in front of the traffic magistrate.

As a teenager, I thought riding bikes was meant to be fun and did not like the idea of bringing traffic rules into the picture. Nevertheless, as I grew up, I realized these incidents had taught us discipline and helped us to lead a meticulous life. We already have the mechanisms of discipline embedded in our genes. It is 'discipline' that has been an immense contributor to our success, be it big or small, despite the odds that we encounter.

These small lessons on discipline that we were taught daily by our father became embedded in us and became part of our personalities. Today I am mentioned as a 'disciplined leader' by my team and also across the healthcare industry; I believe the lessons provided by my father have allowed me to progress in my professional career.

The origin of the discipline that I practice has its roots in our father's lessons since childhood. Whenever I encounter obstacles in my life, an inner voice always reminds me of the disciplined life led by our father.

At first, the sound was confusing, as I have never listened to my innermost Godfather before. Later on, I started listening to this voice, which I believed came from him. During childhood, the lessons provided by my father were my guiding force, and as time passed, my innermost Godfather became my guiding force. Both these voices have been the foundation for all the success that I have attained in my life.

When I look back, I wonder where I would have been if these two guiding forces had not been there with me. In short, I believe that success is synonymous with discipline. Without discipline, success is unattainable.

Hence the first point I would like to discuss with my readers is "success needs discipline." As the old saying goes, *"bear the pain of discipline or take the pain of failure."*

You will not find lines more relevant that link the practice of discipline to success. I would say this is the most pertinent truth as far as success and discipline are concerned.

Self-discipline, the most important characteristic ascribed to leading a successful life, has so many positive outcomes on the lives of individuals. It helps you to stay focused. This focus is needed to reach your goals and to give you the courage to tackle the difficult tasks you encounter in life; focus permits you to defeat the obstacles you face and drives you to attain new altitudes.

**Practice in the Pandemic**

The first wave of COVID-19 caught us all unaware, and by the time we realized it, the entire nation was reeling under its impact. The major caveat that came out of it was that if we are disciplined to practice the suggested preventive measures (masking, hand hygiene, etc.), there is a high chance that we will not catch the highly infectious virus.

However, the lessons learned from this episode were short-lived. We remained disciplined when the incidence of cases was on the rise. Once there was a decline in the incidence, we all went back to our old habits, forgetting all about the practices to prevent the virus spread.

This one factor ensured the occurrence of the second wave, which happened faster than we imagined, and we all are aware of its devastating effects. By virtue of my position, I am not expected to meet each and every patient admitted on a daily basis.

However, during both the waves of the pandemic, when the waves were at their peak, I ensured that I visited every area of the hospital to meet COVID-positive patients and the staff who were on duty in these areas.

My intention was to raise the spirits of the Covid-positive patients and the staff (doctors and nurses) who felt rather demotivated. I wanted them to realize that they are not alone or at the edge in this fight, and I tried to motivate them by making them feel that their seniors are standing with them.

Despite exposing myself to the highly infectious areas, I was fortunate to have remained COVID-negative, primarily owing to one thing: the discipline I was practicing. Whether a small step or a large one, I had all the forbidden habits written in my mind.

I was diligent in following all the 'dos and don'ts.' My innermost Godfather kept reminding me to practice all the necessary steps: using a mask, sanitizing the hands frequently, social distancing, etc.

I was also careful with small actions. I would not touch my face without sanitizing my hands after touching a surface or a door handle; I parked the car myself instead of using valet parking, took the stairs instead of the lift, cleaned the coffee mugs before using them, washed the water bottles in the office before using them, etc. Safety measures must be practiced in the close vicinity as well.

I was careful about not using a common sanitizer bottle after cleaning my hands, scratching or touching my face soon after touching a surface, especially a washbasin or a bucket, discarding the used tissue or mask carelessly, etc. These are just some small examples of the discipline that I had devised for myself and had shared with others as well.

This type of practice requires our minds to be well acquainted with the regulations. Therefore, being disciplined has to be a habit and has to be imbibed in your way of life. I am sure all of you have seen or met astounding and productive leaders and entrepreneurs and have heard inspiring success stories about them. If you evaluate their stories and match some common traits, the most common of all will be **self-discipline**.

You might have the question, what exactly is this self-discipline? Self-discipline can be described as the capacity to control your instincts, reactions, behavior, and emotions. It is what allows you to sacrifice your short-term fulfillment to achieve your long-term pleasure, gratification, and gain. Self-discipline curbs your desire to say 'yes' when you should be saying 'no.' However, it is wrong to state that self-discipline leads to a restrictive and boring life with no enjoyment. It is more about prioritizing self and society than momentary pleasure. Sometimes you may feel troubled while imposing self-discipline; during this time, you must focus on what is important for society as a whole. In short, self-discipline is self-commitment and honesty with yourself.

**Practicing Self-discipline:**

- Self-discipline is a basic part of your character; it allows you to articulate your own identity. H.A. Dorfman, in the book *The Mental ABC's of Pitching*, has mentioned, "*self-discipline is a form of freedom. Freedom from laziness and lethargy, freedom from the expectations and demands of others, freedom from weakness and fear and doubt.*

*Self-Discipline allows a pitcher [person] to feel his individuality, his inner strength, his talent. He is master of, rather than a slave to, his thoughts and emotions"*.

Although people might be highly educated, they are often ignorant of the fact that they are the masters of their own emotions and thoughts.

This ignorance could be a result of the learning they received either at their homes or the educational institutions they went to. It could also result from depressing moods or the inability to overcome the obstacles they encounter in their lives. However, a good understanding of the relationship between self-discipline and character formation would be helpful to climb up the ladder of success.

- Self-discipline is about being most honest and true to yourself. When you become self-disciplined, you start being true to yourself. Self-discipline enables you to see yourself as you are, and not through your whims and fancies. Being true to self has several implications. W.K. Hope has quoted thus: *"Self-discipline is when your conscience tells you something and you don't talk back."* When you sincerely recognize who you are, you would stop talking aloud about many things which were never a part of you.

- Self-discipline is the ability where you control your impulses. As W.K. Hope has mentioned, you will get the power to control your own emotions when you become self-disciplined. Being in control of our impulses is what separates humans from the animal world. It helps us to attain our long-term goals. According to medical science, impulse control is rooted in the brain's prefrontal cortex, which is bigger in humans than in other mammals.

- Self-discipline is the ability to take up and complete tasks that are vital.

Many people do not realize the importance of prioritization. I like to begin my workday early; for me, it is not important whether my workplace (in the past) is at a distance of 55 km, 25 km, or just 5 km.

I aim to reach there by 7:30 am, irrespective of rain, fog, winter, etc. I start my day by completing any routine follow-up work pending from the previous day. I see the various performance matrices that need to be checked daily. I visit either a small or a bigger part of the hospital during this initial part of the day. I schedule my morning meetings according to everyone's convenience, and prior to that, I get my minutes ready.

Keeping in mind everybody's convenience, the meetings are usually scheduled for any time after 9 am. However, punctuality is non-negotiable, and I make it a point to be at the venue at least two minutes early. My morning meetings are never open-ended.

There are key pointers assigned to all the Heads of Department (HODs) and only they are required to speak, mainly reporting on their department's key indicators. Any further discussions on the points are kept for later.

Although 17 to 18 HODs attend these morning meetings, I do not let them extend beyond 20 minutes, so that they can get back to their work and not spend the morning hours sitting in a boardroom. All my meetings and reviews are always on schedule with a preplanned agenda and an upper time limit; this ensures that the discussions remain most productive and to the point, and there is no time wastage for anyone. I ensure that the follow-up for any decisions taken in the meetings or reviews is done based on their priority—routine ones, maybe once a week, and urgent ones, within 24 hours.

I am particular about being well-groomed at work and expect the same from my team as well. (On a couple of occasions, when I found someone sporting a stubble with no genuine excuse, I have given 100 rupees to that person and asked them to get a shave from the nearest barbershop). When I decide on a timeline for a task, I am the hardest on myself about completing the assignment on time. Leading a self-disciplined life has enabled me to prioritize my tasks as per the need. For example, I could very well have reached the hospital only by 10 am or 11 am.

However, my work is my priority, and hence, I follow this schedule every day to make sure that my priorities do not change. These are just some examples of the discipline I follow in my daily working life, irrespective of where I am posted, and as a result, I do not have to make an extra effort to create such discipline in my teams.

Besides knowing me as someone who practices what I preach, the teams also start enjoying it after a while. They see the increase in productivity and the results getting better, and there is no better motivation than results for anyone to make an effort. Self-discipline is a high form of Emotional Quotient (EQ), an imperative trait for any successful person. Self-discipline can sometimes mean turning down instant gratification in favor of long-term success and satisfaction. Successful leaders are found to have a higher EQ.

EQ can be defined as understanding, using, and managing emotions efficiently and positively. However, the relationship between self-discipline and EQ is not known to many people.

## EQ and Self-discipline

Real-life stories of celebrities, academicians, and successful leaders have proven that EQ is directly proportional to self-discipline. Many of them have stated that self-discipline has been very helpful in improving their EQ. American author Daniel Goleman has quoted that *"If your emotional abilities aren't in hand, if you don't have self-awareness, if you are not able to manage your distressing emotions, if you can't have empathy and have effective relationships, then no matter how smart you are, you are not going to get very far."*

This important message has to be passed on to future generations as well. Smartness and success will not be attained unless you are self-disciplined.

Self-discipline is the very foundation for anyone's success.

In most cases, our primary aim in life is to do the right thing. However, we often fail to pull the trigger that allows us to do the right thing, and this trigger happens to be self-discipline. Without pulling this trigger, we will never be able to finish a job.

We could say that self-discipline is the foundation of success. That is why the late motivational speaker, Jim Rohn, has mentioned, *"Discipline is the foundation upon which all success is built. Lack of discipline inevitably leads to failure"*.

The success discussed here is not just the success in the sports field. It also involves your success in business, career, and life, in general.

Self-discipline cannot be developed overnight; you have to work on it. I recently read an interesting quote on self-discipline, or rather on discipline as a whole.

It states, *"you cannot become a disciplined person by choosing to practice self-control once in a while or most of the time. You are going to have to do it all the time."*

We often look at people who have scripted success stories and wonder about their lifestyle; we may even wish to follow the same; however, we forget the hardships that they must have faced to lead a life like that. If you want to learn from someone's success, then you need to learn how they reached the pinnacle from the ache and adversity they had to go through.

You must remember that *Success is a Marathon, Not a Sprint*. Self-discipline is a surety for success; whether it comes early or late, success will definitely come if you practice self-discipline diligently. Self-discipline can sometimes mean turning down instant gratification in favor of long-term success and satisfaction.

I am repeating myself here because this reminds me of a small event from my own life. When I took up the management position, being a doctor, my profile was only limited to Medical Administration as a vertical; this meant that I would not be handling the entire organization by myself, as long as I was in Medical Administration. After a few years in this role, although I was making fast progress in my vertical, I found that the learning curve was not as steep and it was not challenging for me anymore to run only the Medical Administration. I began to dream of having an expanded role in leading the entire hospital. Bitten by the expansion bug, I started getting restless in my present role; my dreams were troubling me, day in and day out. I was already a Medical Director at that particular time, which was the highest position for a Medical Administrator, but I had lost the enthusiasm for this dream position since it seemed too monotonous to me.

The idea of having an expanded role in running the hospital was running through my mind constantly. As a result, without being told by anyone, I started spending time in all the other departments which did not fall under my purview (Finance, Supply Chain, Marketing, Business Development, etc.). I was able to learn quite a lot about all these departments and get an understanding of how they function; I made copious notes of all the knowledge that I was gaining.

This was in 2009 when an opportunity came my way to head the entire hospital in another organization. I was excited about this chance, and after attending various interviews (being interviewed by all their Board Members at different times), I was selected.

However, the challenge here was that this hospital that I was being hired to run was not doing too well, and since I only had Medical Administration experience (till that time), they took me on board at the same level with a commitment to upgrade my position soon as the overall hospital head. The salary offered was the same as what I was getting in my present organization, where I had been working as a Medical Director for a few years. When I informed my present organization about my plans to leave, my CEO made every effort to make me stay back, including giving me a huge jump in my salary.

But my dream was to manage the entire hospital. However, in the new place, I was being offered my old role initially for some time, with a commitment to make me the hospital head very soon; this was actually a huge risk for me.

If my position was not upgraded after I had joined, I would not get a hike in my salary. Until I was made the hospital head, there would not be any financial gain for me. On the other hand, my present organization was increasing my salary out of bounds to retain me. A part of me was wondering why I should move to a new organization that was not doing particularly well. I was not being offered the role I wanted immediately and there was no increase in my salary as well.

However, my EQ, my innermost Godfather, was constantly suggesting that I take a leap of faith into this risky situation and see what happens. Aided by my self-discipline, I gained confidence that I would make it in the new place; I believed that I could turn the hospital around and make it profitable, and thereby earn the position of hospital head, setting my professional journey in motion. I took up the challenge, and I joined the new organization without any salary hike.

I was able to bring in many quick changes there and the organization lived up to its commitment of making me the hospital head (they also provided the salary hike that had been promised). This turned into a big success story not only in my professional journey but also in the history of that hospital, which motivated many other achievers as well. If I did not have confidence in my self-discipline, which consolidated my EQ, I would have never been able to take this huge risk. As a result, I would have remained a frustrated Medical Director throughout these years. Hence, the single most important attribute to becoming successful is self-discipline.

Self-discipline helps you stay focused as you march toward your goals; it gives you the courage to stick with difficult tasks and allows you to overcome obstacles and discomfort as you push yourself to newer heights.

You may find frustrated, unsuccessful people when you look around, both in your professional and personal life. One common factor among them will be that they are not disciplined and cannot control their behavior and their various appetites. Whereas, when you look at the successful people or read about them, you will find that they all possess and practice a higher level of personal discipline. They are the goal-oriented people who have understood the values of the field and practice them.

Some of the major practices followed by successful leaders that involve being disciplined as part of the formula for their success are given below:

- **They are hard-working.** Those who willingly work harder than anyone else are dissatisfied with an average life or result. They crave to test themselves and do not mind working extra hours or going the extra mile to learn something valuable to succeed more. That is why Tim Notke has mentioned, "*Hard work beats talent when talent does not work hard.*" Most of the time, people attribute talent to success; however, more than talent, hard work is the best ingredient needed for being successful in life.

- **They believe in being healthy.** Successful leaders understand the importance of health. Hence, they follow a certain fitness discipline to ensure they are in the best mental and physical frame to drive others and continue to move toward success energetically. I have read an article that was based on research conducted by Harvard University. This research was considered to be one of the longest studies the university has taken up. The team found that success stands synonymous with health. The term 'healthy' implies being happy both physically and mentally.

- **They have a positive mindset.** Various researches have shown clear evidence that happy and composed people are more successful in their lives than unhappy people.

Positivity has a high impact on the performance level, supervision, etc. Successful people develop that control over their mindset, with self-discipline, that they do not let negative thoughts linger on in their minds. They believe in finding a solution for any problem with their self-discipline.

- **They practice being patient.** Blake Powell claimed that without patience, you are dead in the water. He indirectly mentioned that you would not achieve success without being patient.
  Patience is required for every endeavor, and it allows one to realize that it should be a part of you from the beginning of your ambitions. Leaders who have been successful in their respective fields have proved that patience is a 'Mantra' that requires chanting in every second of your life. Successful leaders are aggressive internally. However, their self-discipline and control over themselves create a calm personality, and hence they are patient in attaining the goals. They internally believe in persistence than losing patience.

- **They are always willing.** Success comes with a lot of sacrifices. Sometimes, you might have to let go of the wrong beliefs you possess and move forward with the new set of ideas. However, a willingness to make such sacrifices might not be acceptable to everyone.
  Leaders around us have taught us willingness. They are open to listening, learning, and experimenting and are ready to make sacrifices; this is a high exhibition of self-discipline. Without the willingness to accept change, you might not become a trendsetter.

- **They are always punctual.** Invariably, you will find that successful people value time and are punctual. We need to understand that punctuality is not just about following a time schedule; rather, it is an attitude to respect your commitments. Punctuality is considered one of the important qualities needed in a leader. As a popular quote says, "One thing you cannot recycle is wasted time." Wasted opportunities are lost forever and disrespect to commitments cannot be taken back.

- **They are always organized**. If you look at successful people, you will find that they are highly organized. This organized behavior is visible from the moment you enter their office or their home. It is again visible when you enter into a conversation with them. You will invariably find that they follow a schedule, they are well-prepared on the subject they are conversing about, and they follow an approach that is productive with no wastage of time.
- **They are always accountable.** Successful people hold themselves accountable for completing their tasks and ensure that they stick to their timelines; also, they do not complete a task just for the sake of completion, but bring added value to the job. Moreover, if they fail, they accept the failure and try to do much better the next time, and they do not believe in passing the accountability or blame to someone else.

The best part about discipline is, anyone can develop it. It does not require any training, and it is not complicated at all—you need to make the decision and then train yourself with an honest effort. Here is how you can do it:

**Keep Big Goals**

Challenge yourself to achieve bigger goals; this is the first step to reach your major goals. When you feel that you own it, you dedicate yourself to its achievement. The larger the plan, the more dedicated you become. However, do not boast about it. Research has shown that allocating your goals on impulses can decrease the probability of completing them.

Voicing your agenda or strategy to other people, be it your friends or family members, creates a feeling that the big goal has been already accomplished. This deceives your brain, and you start thinking that you have achieved what you set out to do.

Voicing it triggers a flash in the subconscious mind, which ultimately creates a feeling that we have done enough and more to complete our aim, lessening our basic motivation to accomplish the goals eventually. Hence, refrain from voicing out your objective in public. Keep it private and think about it every minute so that your intrinsic motivation will trigger you to achieve the same.

## Keep Your Goals Clearly Defined

Are you aware of the concept of 'SMART' goals? SMART stands for Specific, Measurable, Achievable, Realistic, and Timely. Make sure that your goal can be put together within these five concepts. When you write your big objectives, mention and define what it means to you and what level (action plan) you plan to achieve.

Be specific. For example, if you want to lose weight (your big goal), mention whether your action plan is to go jogging every day to achieve it. If yes, then cite the time and duration for it. Then, again, if you are planning to include dieting in your action plan, add that as well. Try to break down your action plan into smaller steps, which aids in accomplishing the higher goal. Most of our goals are specific, measurable, and realistic. However, many people disregard the other two concepts, achievable and timely. You should set a time limit for achieving this goal, or it might get procrastinated for a long time. If your plan has a time limit, then make sure to complete it within the prescribed time.

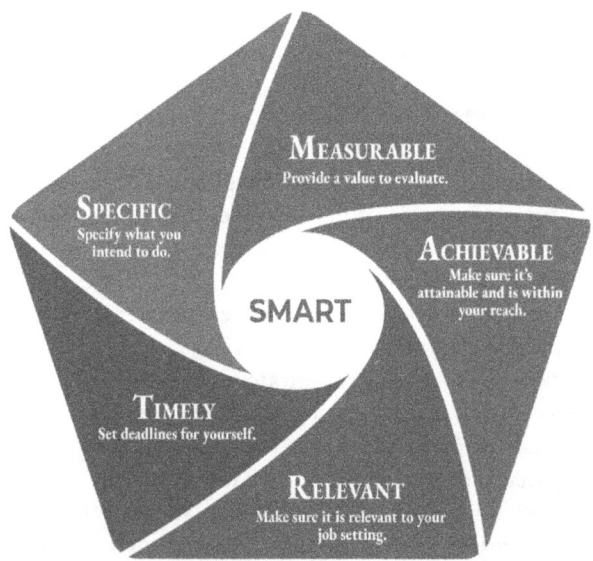

## Daily Movement Toward Your Goal

An athlete will know that if he misses one day's training session, he will fall behind others who would be practicing every day for the competition taking place the next month! That is the undying self-discipline required to be a winner.

Come what may, you must not miss your steps toward your goal and must keep a check on it thrice daily (when you wake, then at noon, and when you go to sleep).

Neeraj Chopra's coach once mentioned that the athlete used to practice his throwing form in every activity he used to do. Many times, his colleagues at the training institute mocked him for that. However, now they have all realized what continuous practice means and why one should ensure a daily movement toward your goal. As the proverb says, "Rome was not built in a day." You cannot achieve your goal if you fail to practice daily.

## Once Started with the Plan, DO NOT STOP

Every day counts for your success. You must not keep changing your plans on every alternate day, even under the influence of others. This is your big goal, and nobody knows how to achieve it better than you. Tell yourself if ever you itch to change, keep moving on, with full force. Never look back after starting a plan because you are not planning to go that way, and looking back might confuse and delude the observer. Always remember that your aim is in the front, and achieving it is your ultimate goal. Never allow anything to come between your journey toward achieving your goal.

## Keep a 'Come What May' Mindset

It is very important to keep reminding yourself that you will accomplish your aim no matter what. This will create positive pressure on yourself and push you. This is called good stress, creating an adrenaline rush stimulating you positively. This also incorporates another message: be bold to take challenges.

If you prefer to stay in your comfort zone and enjoy yourself, you will never get anywhere. I could have enjoyed the hike offered by my hospital rather than taking up the challenges of undertaking the administrative job with lesser pay.

The decision to take up the challenge has made all the difference. Challenges should not be looked at as obstacles but as opportunities. Always remember that often you do not get back the opportunities you lost. Hence, whenever you get a chance, make sure to utilize it and present the best form of yourself.

**Make Routine a Habit**

Without realizing the process, we all have developed certain routines that have become our habits or even reflex actions. For example, before learning to drive a vehicle, remember how jittery you used to feel.

Now, you do not even stop to think about your actions when you drive; every action is by reflex, right from gear change to acceleration or shifting between the accelerator and the brakes. This happens because every action involved in driving first became a habit and then a reflex. Moreover, you are aware that missing out on a reflex can be extremely problematic.

Another example from our life experiences shows how the routine can become a habit. When we get up in the morning, all of us have a specific pattern of activity; some people search for their slippers, some wear their spectacles, and some check their mobiles, to name a few.

Some go straight to the washroom, some have tea first, some drink water, etc., and all these actions are performed without thinking since each of these actions has become a habit now to the concerned person. And if for some reason we miss doing any activity that has become a habit even for a day, we feel strange.

In the same way, if you genuinely work on your self-discipline development plans, one day it will become your habit, and the day you miss acting on your project, you will feel that emptiness, which will ensure that you do not miss it the next day.

I had a friend who was nicknamed 'the clock' in our friend circle. His wife used to comment that even if the clock did not work, she could easily identify the time by her husband's different routine activities.

So, in many cases, the routine gets converted into a habit. If your practice has also been converted into a pattern, then it is a sign that you are very near to achieving your goal.

## Commit Yourself

Discipline is a commitment, a self-commitment, and actually, it is the basis of your success in life, whether personal or professional. Hence, once you want to become disciplined, start by committing to small tasks. Following the steps you have decided upon will help you stay committed. However, there are further several steps that you can take to create a positive change in your life and achieve your goals:

- **Make sure that your plan is complete**: Do not start working on a preliminary plan. A thorough plan will give you a surety of how and when you will accomplish your goal. An incomplete plan would only lead to confusion, and you might stagger away in between.

- **Complete the hardest assignments first:** Many of us tend to start with easy tasks at hand and put the hard ones away. Starting with the hardest assignments will give you a feeling that you have completed the hardest tasks successfully. It also assures that the rest of the work is done easily, giving a boost of confidence.

- **Learn how to schedule your work:** Prioritization is a quality that every individual needs to learn and practice. Scheduling work according to priority helps us understand what needs to be done immediately and what could be done later.

- **Get rid of temptation:** Temptations would be the major obstacles you might encounter in your career. Getting rid of temptations is important to achieve the ambition you have set, as it might divert you away.

- **Do what comes naturally:** Some people find it difficult to start being disciplined, and hence the easy way to start practicing discipline is to do what comes naturally. If you want to become more organized, start concentrating on things that you have already been doing in your life.

For example, if you have the habit of making your bed early in the morning, start doing it in a more perfect way than you have been doing in the past. Slowly, you will be able to achieve your goal.

- **Do not overthink:** Many people give up on their aim when they start thinking that the task, they want to accomplish is tough. Giving up creates chaos as the negative attitude prevents you from reaching anywhere. When I was young, my mother read a story about a King who was afraid of war. He tried to give up whenever he heard that the enemy was approaching. Hence, the army always got defeated in the battle. Without their King, the soldiers were not courageous enough to proceed.
  However, when the King went into exile during such an event, a Swamiji approached him and advised him. After listening to this advice, the King went back and fought the war and became victorious.
  The Swamiji's explanation was very simple. He predicted that the King would only die after 100 years. The King had been afraid of dying early, and that was the reason why he always gave up even before trying to win the war. The moral is to make sure not to overthink and give up on your goal.

- **Hold yourself accountable**: Being accountable for the things that you do is very important. This accountability will help you to have a clear understanding of the goal that you have at hand. For example, if your goal is to study for eight hours a day, make sure to do that. If in between, you gave in to temptation and watched a two-hour movie, not only did you not withstand being tempted but also you are accountable for not achieving your goal. Being responsible and prioritization should be read together, as the first complements the second. That is why Yvonne Acquafredda once stated in an interview that "*It is great to establish goals and create an action plan. However, if there is no accountability built into that process, the effort is likely to fail.*"

- **Write down your progress:** It is very important to keep a journal and write down your progress.

On the least productive day, even a little progress could motivate you as they represent things you have accomplished so far. Also, a journal helps you keep track of the tasks needed to be completed to achieve your goal. Performing tasks during a rough day calls for extra work, and hence when you accomplish it, you feel that the rest of the functions could also be achieved easily. This kind of attitude will help you attain more heights at a faster pace.

- **Know your transition phase**: Once you start, your body and mind will initially resist accepting this change and give you the signal—STOP! However, this is a natural reaction. Do not fall for this, and continue with your discipline for a few weeks. Separate yourself from these initial feelings of laziness or self-pity (yes, at times, this surfaces as well), and keep your long-term goal as a reminder, which you will achieve through this habit of being disciplined. You will see this transforming into a routine.

- **Enjoy your hard work**: Challenge yourself every day to do better than what you did in the previous days. This will make you enjoy your work and lead you to the steps of becoming a self-disciplined leader. Only those activities that we enjoy doing in life can become a sustainable step or habit.

The biggest challenge in a person's journey to becoming self-disciplined is quitting within the initial few weeks. But those who continue to turn self-discipline into a habit, and subsequently into a reflex, are the ones who reach the pinnacle of success in achieving their goals, however tough or big it may have looked initially.

I enjoy being self-disciplined; it makes my life easy and gives me energy and room for improvement. This allows me to keep revisiting and exploring my capabilities and to keep enhancing them. Although it is entirely up to each one of you to choose the life you want to lead, be it a life with or without discipline, goal, or ambition. However, discipline is not boring; it is fun. Discipline is not a prison; it is freedom. It is important to start from the basics to turn your dream into reality and become self-disciplined. For that, first, write the details required in the following table, and fill up your action plans, based on your convenience, as per the steps shown above.

The way to keep reviewing your plan is also mentioned in the table below. (You can create as many of the following tables as you want, but for each goal, keep one table for you to follow easily, and initially, start with just one, to develop yourself into a self-disciplined leader)

| Find your Godfather Inside You | Discipline | Write Here |
|---|---|---|
| Learning Exercise | Write down a specific task or a goal that you are finding difficult to achieve or persist with, despite having started to work on it. OR Any task or goal that you start to work on but fizzles out in between before completing or achieving it | Daily routine or steps you have decided to take to achieve your goal or complete your task in your day-to-day living: |
| | Practice the decided steps every day in the following manner | |
| | Follow-up check for practice thrice daily for ten days – morning, afternoon, night | |
| | Follow-up check for practice twice daily for ten days – morning, night. | |

|  | Follow-up check for practice once daily for ten days, at night. |  |

# 6
# FOCUS
## Channeling your energies, and learning to ignoring shadows to hold to substance

> *"Whenever you want to achieve something, keep your eyes open, concentrate and make sure you know exactly what it is you want. No one can hit their target with their eyes closed."* — Paulo Coelho, The Devil and Miss Prym

**The Eye of the Bird**

We usually think of focus as being in a hyperaware state with the concentration locked onto one aspect. Here are two stories that will help distill the meaning of focus. The first story is about an ambitious disciple. He always wanted to move forward in his learning quickly. However, he felt that his Guru was being unnecessarily slow-paced in teaching him. This made him very restless. One day, he could not hold back and he expressed his desire to finish his learning and move ahead in his life. He expected his Guru to either chastise him or scold him. But he was surprised when the Guru assented to his request. The Guru asked him to come early the next morning.

The student was exultant. He could not wait to find out how his learning could be accelerated. When he reached his school the next day, he found his Guru near the chicken coop. Even as he was trying to understand the scene, his Guru opened the gate to the coop. Squawking loudly, all the chicken rushed out of their enclosure.

As the student stood gasping at this sight, he heard his Guru giving him some instructions, which worsened his mood. His Guru wanted him to catch all the chicken and return them to the coop within an hour. He was jolted into action. He immediately rushed around trying to catch the chicken. He wanted to catch at least a few. But he faced a problem. Even as he stalked a particular chicken, he would find another one that seemed easier to catch. He would shift his target but would end up catching neither of them.

At the end of the appointed hour, he was exhausted. He crumpled to the ground, dejected. Then he saw his Guru come toward him. The Guru said, "You could not catch a single chicken. But, my disciple, worry not; for I shall give you another test. This will be simpler. Can you see that chicken with a red ribbon tied around its neck?" When the student nodded, his teacher then continued, "Catch only that chicken and bring it back to the coop." This time the student was able to catch it quickly as he only looked to catch that particular chicken.

When the student returned, his teacher expounded on the importance of focus. He said, "You need focus to truly learn and understand. Focus is not only our ability to stay clear on what we want to achieve, but it also helps us avoid distractions in our journey toward what we want to achieve."

There is another famous tale in the Mahabharata which tells us the importance of focus. This incident occurred when the Pandavas and Kauravas were being tutored by their Guru, Dronacharya. The story goes that Dronacharya hung a wooden model of a crow on a tree.

The lesson for that day was archery. All the students were equipped with their bows and arrows. They knew the drill and were excited to test their archery skills. However, they were surprised when Dronacharya stopped in front of one of them. He asked the boy a simple question, "What do you see?" He asked the question by pointing toward the bird which was hung on the tree. The boy answered, "I see the tree, the gurukul, and the leaves, flowers, and fruits." Dronacharya shook his head and asked the boy to step back. It was clear that the preceptor did not think that the student was worthy of shooting the arrow. He repeated the same procedure with all the others present. The students gave varying answers. However, their answers did not diverge much from the answer given by the first student.

There were only some minor variations such as one person giving a detailed description or one person being a little vague about the same thing. Dronacharya was patient.

He carefully listened to every answer, and to the waiting students, it seemed like the correct answer had been given each time. However, at the end of their lengthy expositions, he would ask them to step back. Some even went so far as to describe the intangible. They saw some leaves flutter due to the breeze and they described the wind.

Finally, Dronacharya stood in front of Arjuna. When the same question was posed to Arjuna, he answered, "I see the bejeweled eye of the wooden crow." Dronacharya simply replied, "Let loose your arrow." Arjuna put the arrow on his bow and pulled the string back and let loose with a twang.

To no one's surprise, Arjuna had hit the eye of the crow. That is the true nature of focus. It is not just about looking at the end goal. It is also about not getting distracted by the sideshows that may accompany you on the journey to achieving that goal. Although the word focus may be spelled with just five letters, it has great implications.

Focus is at the root of the creation of many wonders, the accomplishment of impossible feats, and the greatest turnarounds. Look at any success story and you will find focus as one of the driving principles behind it. Why? Think of a stage play. Let us say there are many characters on the stage for a particular scene. Suddenly, the lights dim and the spotlight falls on one character. It is easy to understand that at this juncture the focus is on the speech or actions of that particular character. We are not concerned about the others during this time. Put simply, focus helps you ignore everything else and ensures that you are on the correct path. It helps you eliminate distractions. The greatest benefit of focus is that it helps you move forward. Even when you stumble, if you are focused, you will find that you can get up easily, dust yourself off, and move toward your goal.

Let us take the simplest analogy. You wake up in the morning and you know that you have to be at your office or workplace by a certain time. You could have an important client meeting. All your actions from when you wake up would be geared toward that. You know that you have to complete your morning ablutions in so many minutes.

You would allocate another set number of minutes to have your breakfast and get ready. You could also allocate some time to go over your documents and presentation for the last time to be prepared for that meeting. If you are traveling by your personal vehicle, you will know the time you have to start to beat the traffic. Now ask yourself this question. Would you spend time with your neighbor at this point to indulge in some gossip? Let us move on to the road. You would know the shortest route to your office. Now ask yourself a few more questions. Would you stop at every tea stall for a cup of tea? Would you be distracted by a new advertisement hoarding? Would you take a circuitous route to the office? Would you explore a new by-lane you have not seen before? Your answers to all these questions would be in the negative.

If you encounter any emergency, you will be even more hard-pressed for time and you will move accordingly. If you were going to a new place, you would rely on Google Maps. Even if technology fails, you would find yourself walking up to strangers and asking them for directions to your destination. Why? You are focused on reaching your destination in time and you will not allow yourself to be bothered by any of these distractions.

This is the magic of focus. We do not even realize it, but we need the trait 'focus' in so many of our daily activities. But we do not acknowledge it as we tend to think of these activities as trivial. We do not think of them in the same breath as our long-term goals and objectives. However, the key point to note here is that we already have this essential trait of focus. The challenge now is to translate this focus to all the activities we undertake to help us achieve all our short-term and long-term goals.

There would have been occasions when you wanted to be focused, but got distracted by something too big to ignore. This is a common complaint that many of us have faced. But when you are truly focused, nothing can distract you, big or small, because the focused 'you' will be an unstoppable juggernaut!

## Silence in Spite of Sonorous Speakers

T.N. Seshan was the Chief Election Commissioner of India from 1990 to 1996. He initiated many electoral reforms during his tenure. One of the changes that he instituted was the ban on loudspeakers and other noisy forms of canvassing during elections.

Prior to this reform being put into practice, election time also meant cacophonous times. It was during one such election that my fourth-year MBBS exams were being held.

I am sure everyone has indulged in some idiosyncrasy or superstitious practice during their exam preparations. My idiosyncrasy was that I used to sit at one particular study table, just behind my room's balcony. The additional part of this mandate was that the balcony door had to be open. I found that I was able to study far better when I followed this practice. It was a pattern that worked for me and I did not want to change it.

However, for this particular exam, it seemed like the political parties did not intend to give us any peace. There were three loudspeakers placed outside. All of them were facing my balcony! It sounded like they were 'turned up to eleven' and they constantly blared for 24 hours. The din was so loud that some of us feared that our eardrums would burst. However, I never strayed from my practice when it came to my study. I opened the balcony door and studied.

If I had to speak to someone even standing two feet away, I had to scream at the top of my voice to be audible. But when it came to my studying, I was somehow able to tune out the noise. I remember my brother trying to close the door. But I stopped him. He was angry and demanded that the door be closed and that I move elsewhere to study. I was adamant and I won that argument by sheer force of my will.

I never realized that I was actually practicing the highest level of focus at that particular time. My focus on my studies did not let me care about any noises. Amidst all that chaos, I managed to focus on my studies, and when the results were out, I had come out with flying colors as well! This is a small example that has served to remind me in the subsequent years and continues to remind me that if you are focused, nothing can deter you from achieving what you want to in life. There are many benefits when it comes to being focused. One of them is that you will be efficient. When you rule out distractions, you pay your whole attention to the task that needs to be done. So, when you are focused on your task, you will plan for your goal.

This means that you will be ready to face any challenge or obstacle. You will have a contingency plan ready and will be prepared for any shift.

## Flow of Focus

When you are focused, you also produce a better quality of work. When you shift your focus constantly, your work will also reflect it. When you are focused on one task, you will look to complete it quickly and without any mistakes. If you are distracted, it is possible for you to make a simple mistake and not know that you have erred. Only when you are focused will you notice these details.

Another crucial benefit of being focused is that you will be less stressed. When you are not focused, your work ends up lagging, and this could lead to your feeling overworked and overwhelmed. The side-effect of this is that you end up being negative-minded. You will be constantly trying to catch up and this could lead you to second-guess yourself. When you are focused, you will look at your productivity and be more positive-minded. Your determination and your self-confidence will grow. You will learn to trust yourself.

The crucial part of being focused is that you send a signal to your subconscious mind that you want to complete a certain task. Your subconscious mind then actively works to help you complete your task. Say, for example, you want to write a blog post with some cogent arguments. Even as you write the introduction, your subconscious mind will start organizing your thoughts for the paragraphs that will follow. It will help you proceed further without any hesitation. This connection with your subconscious mind will allow you to have a better understanding of yourself. It will be the making of you and you will only grow.

## Recognition in the Raucousness

I remember an incident from my first-year MBBS at the Government Medical College in Jammu. It was the year 1990 and I had come to Delhi as a part of my college team to participate in PULSE, which is a famous annual inter-medical college event held at AIIMS, New Delhi. It is a typical college fest with cultural, sports, and other fun events and competitions. Sanjay, my teammate, and I had registered ourselves to participate in an event called Matka Jhatka.

The basic idea of this competition is that a blindfolded contestant has to break a pitcher which is hung up on a tree or a pole, using a stick.

The other teammate is supposed to shout out the instructions and guide the contestant to the spot where he can swing the stick to break the pitcher. The teammate cannot, however, touch or guide the blindfolded contestant through any other means. The fastest team to achieve this task will win the game.

But the game is not that straightforward. Each blindfolded person will be led to a random spot to begin the game, which means prior memorizing of the directions would be useless. To complicate matters, you also have a raucous crowd who will be shouting out their instructions to further confuse the contestant. That year the event was being held at a basketball court and it was surrounded by 500 screaming people.

The pitcher was hung up on one of the rims of the basket. Sanjay opted to be blindfolded, thus making me the guide. We were part of the crowd and we saw other contestants.

There were innumerable examples of people being led astray by the noise of others. Some were even just a swing away from breaking the pot when a voice from the crowd led them in the wrong direction! It was a laugh riot and we had so much fun. The crowd played its part. They would be silent at the start and then a buzz would start as the contestant made their way forward. As soon as they were near the 3-point line of the basket, the noise would erupt, shocking and deafening the blindfolded contestant.

Sanjay and I wanted to win the game! As I looked at all the contestants, I was sure how the contest could be won. I told him to focus on my voice from the moment he was blindfolded. Since he would only hear my voice when the whistle blew, I asked him to recognize my voice and focus only on that.

Even when the buzz from the crowd grew, he should only focus on my voice. I told him that I would be speaking throughout the entire time until he breaks the pot. It was a wonderful strategy and we broke the pot in three minutes! That time was not topped by anyone and we came in first in that competition. From this story, we can sum up what a focused approach can achieve:

- It will ensure your victory.
- It will ensure you reach your goal.
- It will ensure that no distraction can deter you.
- It will give you strategies to reach your destination or your goal.

## Moving Perspectives

One of the most pivotal times of my life was when I shifted from Udaipur to Delhi. I had been working as a clinician in Hindustan Zinc Limited, which was a government company, in Udaipur. It was an extremely comfortable job. I am not referring to the nature of my job, but to the added benefits. I was able to provide a wonderful house as accommodation for my family. The job was secure and the campus was huge with all the amenities.

My workplace, the hospital, was just a few steps away (about 200 meters) from my doorstep. I left all these comforts to move to Delhi. However, there was a just reason for the move. My wife had moved to Delhi when she was pregnant with our second child. She had just finished her specialization in Medicine and had been unable to find a good position in Udaipur. She was offered a job in a big organization in Delhi and had to move there. Fortunately, the organization also provided accommodation for families. My daughter too moved with her as it is important for a child to stay with her mother. The plan was that I would visit on holidays and weekends and spend time with them. We continued this routine for a few months. However, we soon found it was taking a toll on us. We realized that this occasional meet-up was not good for the family. We played around with this idea for a while.

However, it took concrete shape when our son was born in 2004. But this time, it was my turn to not find any lucky breaks. There were no jobs available for my profile. It was at this moment that someone suggested a management role. I was worried as I did not have a management background. But I was intrigued by the challenge and I knew that I had to avail that opportunity to stay with my family. There was an opening for the post of Assistant Medical Superintendent at a private hospital.

I appeared for the interview and I could see that those interviewing me were impressed with my answers. I was wondering when the tough questions would be asked. They had some doubts over the appeal of the job to me. I had a well-paying secure government job. Why would I want to move to a private enterprise? I tried assuring them that if given the opportunity, I would take it. They continued to have this doubt even when they offered me the job. They asked me to write a check for an amount equal to the agreed-upon salary.

The check would be returned to me on the first day I reported for the job. This was their way of getting material assurance from me. Well, I did provide them with the check and it was indeed returned to me on my first day at work. However, I had no time to rest. Even as I was treading water in my new position, people around me were warning of the sharks. They told me that job survival depended upon the network of connections I could build up.

I was told that I needed to have a good relationship with the trustees and management if I wanted to stay on in the job. I was warned that my performance would not count, and that I had to start looking for a new job immediately. I was shocked as I was just moving into a new field and a new place. I had gotten the job with no reference. So, my situation appeared to be that of a man stuck alone on a ship in stormy waters with no clue on how to sail it.

I was insecure and felt immeasurable pressure daily. I was stressed and second-guessed every decision I made fearing it would be my last. I was scared of committing a mistake. However, after a few days, I realized that I was doing myself no favors with such an attitude.

I was not being 'me' and consequently I was unhappy. So, I took the time to reflect and evaluate my position. Even as I was analyzing what I could do, I suddenly remembered the lessons I learned from my parents. I remembered my father's words. He had once told me, "Never ever have negative thoughts about your workplace or country and never do them any harm. The workplace is what provides you your bread and butter and your country is where you were brought into the world and hence your identity."

When I thought along those lines, I realized that I had lost my focus. I was dreading to face the day instead of preparing for it. I knew if I had to face the challenges at my workplace, I needed to be focused on my job and not spend my time fearful of the potential pitfalls.

This perspective changed the game for me. I found my confidence again. I was back to the normal 'me'. Now I spent all my working hours and sometimes more to nail down the aspects of my job. I was now driven by the need for excellence. So, my focus was entirely on learning the basics of my new job. Since my motto was not to focus on the negative aspects of my job, my integrity toward it also started to peak. I had become a different 'me'. After a few days, I realized something. I was enjoying my job.

I loved the challenges that came my way and due to my recovered confidence, I was fearless when it came to doing things that were required for the organization. I soon noticed that this had a positive impact on the people around me. There was respect, recognition, and even appreciation. Whenever there were difficult assignments, the trustees told my colleagues that I would be more suitable to handle such assignments.

I would only know of this fact much later in my career. As I mentioned in an earlier chapter, we worked in rotational shifts and nothing fazed me. I put in the same intensity and focus into my job, no matter what shift it was. I quickly became the best performer and was rewarded with a fixed shift during general times. I got this role due to the recommendation of my CEO. However, I had not known the CEO for more than a few months and we had never had any personal interactions. He recommended the role based on the quality of my work.

That was the moment when it dawned on me that I had been given this choicest role purely because of my work and not any connections. It showed me the error of my ways in my early days under stark lighting. I realized that one must not rely on the words of others to evaluate a situation.

The best-case scenario would be to follow the example of Walt Whitman, who said, "*Be curious, not judgmental.*" So, find the facts for yourself and analyze them. There is no shortcut to success. It needs confidence, positive thinking, hard work, and focus.

After a few years, I was offered an opportunity in another organization. It was a chance I could not turn down. When I communicated my decision to my employers, they left no stone unturned in trying to retain me. Just think about this situation. When I joined the organization, people told me that I would not last long as I had no references or connections with the trustees and the management. I was warned that it would be one strike and I would be fired. But here I was a few years later, and the very same organization did not want me to leave. This was such a heartening victory for my hard work and the basics learned over the years!

However, I apologized to them. The other opportunity provided me the chance to work from the project phase, which was not available at the present organization. I wanted that chance as I knew that I would learn something new and vital from it. So, we parted on good and affectionate terms.

However, the depth of affection and respect I had built over there was only revealed seven to eight years after my leaving. I was admitted to the same hospital for a medical emergency. As I was getting admitted, I did not recognize any of the staff as they all seemed new. But one of the housekeeping staff saw me and recognized me. He came and touched my feet and asked about my health. He then spread the word around. In the following hours, the CEO and the top trustees paid a visit to enquire about my health.

Even the staff who knew me paid a visit to the ward where I was admitted. So, when I started my journey in management as an Assistant Medical Superintendent, after a brief period of insecurity, I knew that I had to be focused. I knew that once I had decided to move on this path, only my focus would help me navigate this new territory. I also knew that I could not just stay stagnant in the same position for life. I had to hone my skills and enhance my knowledge. I also subsequently completed a post-graduate course and I learned on the job from my seniors. The undeniable ingredient required to achieve all of these was focus. I needed it so that I would not just survive, but thrive.

If you want to thrive in the professional world or in any entrepreneurial adventure, it is not enough if you have the desire and gumption for it. You need a number of other factors like a learning mindset, reasoning power, problem-solving capacity, clear and appropriate thinking, and a set decision-making process. You need all of these to succeed. You need focus to properly integrate all these factors within your mindset. You could say focus is the gateway to rationality, effectiveness, and success.

This quality of your focus is even more important when you are in a leadership position. Just imagine a scenario where you are working for a boss who is haphazard when it comes to issuing instructions or directives. But you are expected to deliver the results within a proposed timeline.

There may be occasions when you are given some vital information required to complete the job much later than needed. It would mean a lot of overtime work and working at the last minute to fill in the gaps. Would you like working under such a boss? Would you be satisfied with your work?

Thus, it is vital as a leader that you instill a focus-driven approach. Set an example from the top. You will then find that your team also follows and functions in the same way.

You have to remember that you have not been made a leader to just boss around; you have been made a leader to lead. It is not a privilege; it is a responsibility. You have to influence the work culture positively. Take any top performer or successful leader. They are highly focused on their goals. They talk of how they act as if they have blinders on. They plan and schedule to tackle big issues and do not let any distractions lead them down unwanted tangential routes. I shall list some of these behaviors and habits of these people. Compare and see where you can improve your focus.

1. **No gossip:** There is a popular adage that says thus: "Great minds discuss ideas; average minds discuss events; small minds discuss people." Focused people avoid gossiping as there are far more productive things they wish to do with their time. Generally, people who gossip are motivated by feelings of inadequacy and jealousy. It is an indication of shallow behavior due to unfulfilled personal or professional lives.

2. **No multitasking:** Just imagine a scenario where you are multitasking. On which task is your mind focused on the most? By focusing too much on one activity, would the other task be compromised? Focused individuals understand that multitasking would generally mean a compromise to any or all the tasks that are being done together! Hence, they are clear multitasking is more detrimental than beneficial. They believe in focusing on one thing as it results in the best productivity.

3. **No procrastination:** The character Mr. Micawber in the book David Copperfield written by Charles Dickens makes this remark: *"Procrastination is the thief of time, collar him."* However, the original quote is attributed to the English writer Edward Young. Focused individuals may shift their tasks around due to certain priorities. However, you will never find them in a state of last-minute panic. There is no rush at the eleventh hour as a result of postponed tasks. They ensure that their tasks are done when they need to be done. Even if they feel tired, if they have set a deadline to finish a task, they will push themselves to get it done.

4. **No distractions:** There can be many distractions. The notification of a message or an application on the phone can divert your attention. Receiving e-mails can be a distraction. Focused individuals are aware of these distractions and they work accordingly so that they do not get distracted. For instance, they may check their e-mails at an allotted period in the morning and reply to the relevant ones; any further e-mails they receive are ignored until they have completed the tasks they set for themselves.

5. **No validation:** Focused individuals concentrate more on how they can contribute to the work or task at hand to increase its value. They do not distract themselves by looking for the approval of others. When they do the tasks as planned, they know that they have done their jobs. Their integrity and the added value to the work suffice their need for self-worth. Thus, they never seek any validation or approval from others as they are clear about their self-worth. The only time they seek any opinion from others is when the task demands so, like an opinion poll or feedback about a process, etc.

6. **Be organized:** As mentioned earlier, focused individuals are meticulous when it comes to scheduling time. They cannot stand disorganization. Chaos is not useful for productivity and it could encourage malaise. It blocks creativity and can cost valuable time. Thus, they ensure that everything is in order and there is no wastage of time or resources.

7. **No excuses:** Focused people are believers in the adage "where there is a will, there is a way." They believe in finding a way to accomplish their tasks and do not believe in finding nonsensical excuses to avoid a task. They do not wait for a perfect time and perfect conditions. They believe they can shape the time and conditions to the way they desire.

8. **Take calculated risks:** Focused individuals are learners. They know that they will only learn from taking chances. They know they have to take calculated risks to learn.

They are not gamblers. But they know how to push just enough relying on their confidence and capability. They know that if they do not push, they will stay stagnant and safe. They take calculated risks with the intent of learning from both the positive and negative outcomes.

9. **No rash reactions:** They do not believe in rushing into anything. They believe in quick analysis and thinking through before deciding the next best step.

10. **Mind their own business:** Focused people believe in minding their own business. They believe there is no need to get into other people's work, unless they are specifically called. They are clear about where they have to contribute and work toward it. This attitude is also related to how they avoid gossiping.

11. **No comparison with others:** Comparing oneself to others is a waste of time. Comparisons can demoralize you and leave you with an inferiority complex. Focused individuals concern themselves with how they can add value and not how they stack up against others.

12. **No "Yes" man:** On a related note, focused individuals focus on their goals and not on how they can please others. There may be occasions where you say, yes due to several reasons. You could feel coerced by your peers or bosses. Sometimes you may say yes even when you know it could affect productivity adversely. But you give your assent because you feel that you cannot disappoint someone. However, focused individuals know when to be firm and polite and say no, especially when it compromises their values and productivity.

13. **No running away:** They are not quitters. They know that only those people who are not focused quit when things get tougher. They let the fear of failure drive their eyes away from the prize. Focused individuals practice this common adage—When the going gets tough, the tough get going!

These 13 behavioral attitudes will give you an idea of how focused you are and also point out where your deficiencies could lie. Do not worry if you feel that you fall short on any one of these attitudes. If you are committed to improving yourself on any of these traits, it will be easy.

The ease comes from ensuring that this desire to be more focused is ingrained into your daily life. When you make focus a central tenet of your life, you will be successful, no matter what. Look no further than Thomas Edison.

He enlightened us with his focus to make the light bulb despite the many failures. He learned from his mistakes and focused on making the incandescent light bulb. It was his focus that ensured that even after 1000 missteps, he could finally invent the light bulb. That is the power of focus.

However, when I say you have to be focused on your productivity, I do not mean that you only focus on productivity to the exclusion of all else in your life. There are some situations that may seem like distractions, but they are important elements of your life. For example:

- Relationships (marriage, children, siblings, parents, etc.)
- Spending time with friends
- Checking on important e-mails or messages
- Attending important calls
- Surfing the internet for reading important materials

These are all vital parts of your life and are important to your development. You need to also spend time on these elements. However, it does not mean that you veer toward any extreme.

Do not be only focused on your work or only focused on these elements. It would be like boiling water in an uncovered pot. The water will evaporate after some time leaving you empty and unfulfilled. You have to find a balance and schedule your life so that you have time for these personal moments as well as professional production. There are a few points that I want to highlight at this juncture.

When you start working toward improving your focus, you should know what your distractions are. Keep them in mind and plan accordingly. As mentioned previously, avoid multitasking.

Even if you think that you are a master multitasker, there will be some loss in quality when you juggle between two tasks or more. Finally, ensure that you never leave a task midway. When you interrupt your concentration, you will find it harder to resume your task from the same state of concentration again. So, focus wholeheartedly on the task you are presently doing and not on the tasks done before or yet to come. This leads me to a couple of pertinent questions:

## Can You Become More Focused? Can You Improve Your Focus?

The simple answer to both these questions is, yes. However, you cannot just wish to be more focused. It requires commitment. The first step is to identify that you need to improve your focus. You would have become aware of the need to improve your focus after reading the 13 behavioral traits of focused individuals. Here are the steps you should follow to improve your focus:

1) Your Focus Area
2) Devise the Steps to Reach Your Goal
3) Get Set Go

1. **Your focus area:** It is important that you first list the goal or task that you wish to accomplish. Write it down. It is also essential that this activity should be a challenge with the possibility that your focus may be diverted. Once you write it down, plan a tentative timeline to accomplish this goal.

2. **Devise the steps to reach your goal:** Once you have your goal and proposed timeline, have a set of milestones to achieve this goal. So, for instance, if you have a goal to be accomplished in 3 days, have milestones and checkpoints as to how much should be completed by the end of day 1 and day 2. These are the steps you need to plan and look to achieve. Essentially, you are breaking down your bigger goal into smaller steps so that you are not deterred by the long-term goal. It is about managing your ambitions. So, have these additional stepwise timelines that work toward your bigger timeline.

3. **Get Set Go:** There is nothing else left now. Just go out and do it. You have the 'get', which is the setting of the larger goal, and 'set', where you have planned the milestones. You are now at the start line. So, go and ensure that you work diligently and remain focused on the finish line.

While I have discussed in great detail about focus from the angle of productivity, I also need to bring to your attention some elements of your life that need care. These elements or actions are necessary to work with full focus. Pay attention to these actions and plan them into your schedule.

1. **Rest:** It is extremely important that you provide rest to your body and mind. Even a machine needs time to rest and cool down.
You have to ensure that you get the right amount of sleep. If you get enough sleep, you will wake up fresh and raring to go! I have a personal experience to share to highlight the importance of rest. I had an internal examination during my MBBS days. On the eve of the exam, I was still revising a few concepts and I was not ready. Hence, I decided to stay awake the whole night and finish my preparations.

I planned to study well, then write the examination the next morning. The idea was that I would sleep after the examination. I can tell you that it was not a smart plan. When I sat down for the examination, my lack of rest was telling. My head was spinning and I could barely remember the last-minute details I had crammed during the night. I had snatches of information, but I could not recollect any details with clarity. I had such a severe headache trying to muster my mental strength that I thought my head weighed more than the rest of my body! Needless to say, I fared terribly in that examination. The saving grace was that it was an internal examination and I had another test in that same subject to make up the deficit caused by this test. This experience taught me the importance of rest.

2. **Best time:** Focused individuals do not believe in the perfect time or conditions. However, they are aware of the period when they are the most productive. Find your time and stick to it. Do not be swayed by the advice of others. Find the time when you are most productive and feel creatively inclined.

   Choose that time for your appropriate task. I shall share another personal experience. I was made aware that exercising in the morning was most beneficial for one's health. I regularly exercise, and so I thought that I should do my exercising in the mornings. When I was in my teens, I noticed something. I was missing out on my daily exercises ever since I had decided to exercise in the mornings. I realized that I was not a morning person, and this made it difficult to follow a morning exercise schedule. Hence, I shifted my exercise time to the evening and I found that I was able to stick to it. Even today, I exercise in the evenings.

3. **Know your conditional distractions:** Some of you may have an 'ideal scenario' syndrome, which means before you sit to work, you want your house to be clean, a cup of tea next to you, or a bottle of water to drink by your side (it can be any list).

   These are your conditional distractions. There are two ways to handle these.

Either you get over these and do not let them matter, or just have a time fixed to attend to these before you start on your task. If you do not adopt either of these methods, these small tasks will cause procrastination.

4. **Right space:** On a related thought, whatever space you feel is best for you, just use that for your focused task work. Some people may prefer a clean desk, while a kitchen table might suit others—it can be any place for anybody. If you remember from my story, I had a table near the balcony. If you find a spot that makes you feel focused, do not hesitate to use it. Even if it means driving down to your office on an off-hour or holiday, do it.

5. **Mind your notifications:** While it is easier said than done, these are some of the most important distractions to get over with! You could get notifications like an e-mail or a phone call from your partner, children (though affectionately), colleagues, etc. Find a way to deal with these notifications so that they do not bother you. If you are expecting a call or a message from a human connection, let them know of a time when you will be available. Plan it in your schedule.

6. **Coffee works:** While working on a lengthy task, taking a coffee break for five minutes works well as it can bring back your focus to the task on hand.

7. **Avoid being a 'Squirrel':** Squirrels typically cannot focus, and hence keep jumping from one spot to another. Ensure that you do not drift: not just physically but also mentally. People who have the habit of abruptly jumping from one idea to another or one project to the next are unfocused. Such a lack of focus may even become detrimental to your confidence and impact your productivity in getting things accomplished.

8. **Creativity first**: When you are planning your overall roadmap, ensure that the creative aspects of the tasks are done at the start of the day.

Creativity needs greater focus than the mechanical component of a task. So, keep the first phase of the day for your creative work. If you keep it to the later parts of the day, you could be tired and exhausted when you come to that aspect. It would impact your creativity.

These small, practical daily guidelines will definitely help you in your journey to becoming more focused, thus helping you to become more productive, and as a result, more successful.

Based on what has been discussed above, now is the time to get into the real 'Get Set Go'! So, go ahead, use the following table, and start your journey to becoming more focused as a person and a professional!

| Find Your Godfather Inside You | Focus | Write Here |
|---|---|---|
| Learning Exercise | Write down a goal that you want to achieve, with full focus. | Sub-steps that you have decided to follow in your day-to-day life to complete this task, with timelines:<br>1.<br>2.<br>3. |
| | | 'The Important Sides' (please see above) you want to consider, as you start your focused journey:<br>a.<br>b.<br>c.<br>d.<br>e.<br>f.<br>g.<br>h. |
| | Practice the decided sub-steps every day, in the following manner | |
| | Follow-up check for | |

|  | practice thrice daily for 10 days – morning, afternoon, and night |  |
|--|--|--|
|  | Follow-up check for practice twice daily for 10 days – morning and night |  |
|  | Follow-up check for practice once daily for 10 days, at night |  |

# 7
# RESPONSIBILITY & ACCOUNTABILITY
## Gardening your soul with ownership

*"Responsibility to yourself means refusing to let others do your thinking, talking, and naming for you; it means learning to respect and use your brains and instincts; hence, grappling with hard work."* – Adrienne Rich

### A Mother's Legacy

I have narrated the story earlier of how we learned about our father's demise. My brothers and I were still studying, and some of us were in school. The incident turned our lives upside down, and the world we knew ceased to exist. All we had before us was darkness.

Upon retrospection, I have realized that our situation was far direr than what I had known then. My father was an honest judge, and we were dependent on his salary. Hence, as a large family, his salary was just about enough for our sustenance. We had no savings to fall back on, and since we had lived in government accommodations, we were left with no roof above our heads. We had no home we could call our own and retrieve our roots. In a day, we lost the umbrella that shielded us from the harsh realities of the world, and we lost the heart that gave us stability. Our maternal uncle came forward and helped us with a residence. In this appalling situation, the one who became the greatest savior was our mother; she stepped up to fill in the void.

We knew that our mother was equally devastated after losing her husband, her partner. But she had never let us see that side. She had lived her life as a homemaker. As I have mentioned, that day transformed my mother and made her strong and assured. I could see the sheen of tears in her eyes, but her voice never wavered. She gave us the warmth and support we needed. In the darkness that abounded, she became the beacon for us to move forward. When she said, "I will be your father and your mother. Your father has entrusted me with the responsibility to see that you grow up well and are cared for. I will ensure that to the best of my ability," it soothed our grieving hearts.

The incident tamed my childhood waywardness. My father has taught me many things, but my mother demonstrated courage and responsibility on that day. Even as she grieved, she knew she had to get up and walk for us and lead the way. Those words were not merely words; since that fateful night, she became the embodiment of them.

She brought us up never compromising with family values, and we learned from her. I knew that 'responsibility' is not a catchphrase; it is the founding stone in making a person during the toughest of circumstances. I used to be an impertinent and irresponsible kid, but I changed, perceiving how our mother carried us, held us, protected us, and shielded us at every step until we settled in our lives. We missed our father, but our mother made sure that we never felt his absence.

She taught me about responsibility at such an early stage of my life. She has always inspired me to exhibit responsibility at every professional and personal step to improve my career and life. Why is it important to be responsible? If you are not accountable, you cannot progress in life. It will be visible in your behavior, dealings, and actions. If you are irresponsible, none can trust you. There will be times when you will be asked to step up in life. Recalling a line from Hubert Selby Jr.'s Requiem for a Dream: "*Eventually we all have to accept full and total responsibility for our actions, everything we have done, and have not done.*" I have learned responsibility at an early age from the biggest setback ever imagined by a young boy. It is the steel-like frame of a seemingly frail woman who stood firm protecting us as the winds of vicissitudes threatened to blow us all over. I remember my mother every time I fell short. I learned the trait of responsibility from none but my mother.

**Understanding Responsibility**

Let us now explore the idea of responsibility. Modern popular culture will pitch in a famous line from the Spiderman movie associated with power. It almost suggests that it is a burden. However, it could not be farther from the truth.

Responsibility is not about the load but the love and concern you have toward others. If we were to explore the word in common parlance, we would associate it with marriage, parenthood, education of children, etc. We tend to think of the biggest milestones in life as the different forms of responsibility. Although there is no doubt regarding the same, in a simpler sense, responsibility is a habit. It is a part of your character. Responsibility makes you do things exactly when it is supposed to be done. This definition applies to all types of works, whether small or big. Responsibility implies you complete the task immediately instead of postponing. If you are responsible, you will feel uncomfortable when you leave your job unfinished. Responsibility is a commitment to yourself.

If you wish to be a leader, there is no greater requirement than being responsible. When you think about it, punctuality, time management, leading from the front, planning, etc., are the essential traits of a leader. All of these can be traced to just one fundamental idea: responsibility. When you think of it in personal terms, it also means taking care of yourself or a loved one during a crisis. Hence, embrace this trait and inculcate it in your daily life. You will find that when you exhibit responsibility, you will enhance your productivity and boost your self-esteem. Your relationships, both in the professional and personal world, will improve manyfold. If you are responsible, you can be sure of the following benefits in the longer run:

- Responsibility ensures a sense of purpose.
- Responsibility creates an ability to respond appropriately and not be panicked into knee-jerk reactions.
- Responsibility allows you to stay prepared.
- Responsibility implies planning and finding solutions for challenges.
- Responsibility keeps you ready to face any uncertainty with confidence, keeping it under your control.

- Responsibility lets you let go of uncontrollable things and lets you discard distractions.
- Responsibility insinuates adaptability.
- Responsibility provides a direction for building resilience in adversity.
- Responsibility purports surety for success.

One of the more recent examples where our sense of responsibility helped was during the second wave of COVID 19. It was an extremely trying time. I remember that my hospital like many others was struggling with the shortage of oxygen. We also suffered from a lack of beds. However, the greater need of the hour was oxygen. My team and I brainstormed and we found a solution. Our method was then replicated with varying degrees of success by other hospitals. We searched for every avenue to source oxygen. My team members did not complain about the long hours of work. All of us worked to find a solution.

The gamechanger was when one of the staff found that we could source oxygen from another state, but getting a truckload of oxygen cylinders would take us three days. We planned and decided to use three trucks, and each would leave on three consecutive days. Thus, on the fourth day, the first truck would be back and then make its sojourn on the fifth day when the second truck returned, and a similar plan would be followed by the third truck. The rotation would ensure that we had fresh oxygen supplies daily except for the first three days. We had also figured out how to ration our remaining supplies for those three days. I was automatically taking up responsibility personally, but the same was true for the rest of the staff as well. None of us needed an alarm to check on the oxygen supply status every 90 minutes.

When I was at home, I started sleeping in the living room on the sofa, as my cellular network coverage was weaker in my bedroom. I knew that I could not afford to miss a single call. These are the smaller things we did as if they were ingrained. Everyone did their part voluntarily without being told.

So, are there any symbolic peculiarities of responsibility? Yes, there are some very basic steps you could follow to ensure that you are responsible. These apply to any situation.

- Plan ahead
- Keep tight control over any given situation
- Anticipate possible obstacles
- Delegate instead of micromanaging
- Constantly check the progress
- Ask for help whenever needed
- Foster a tough mentality

"*Accountability breeds response-ability.*" – Stephen R Covey

**Understanding Accountability**

In 2007, I was in Medical Administration in my previous organization, just before I joined another hospital to take charge of the entire hospital. The role in Medical Administration was limited to clinical matters: doctors, clinical processes, clinical quality, etc. Other departments like Finance, HR, Purchase and Supply Chain, Operations, etc., were not a part of my remit. However, I had the dream of running the entire show myself one day. So, I used to take an interest in the functions of these departments.

As part of the job, I used to have weekly reviews with other administrators and department heads and with the CEO. The CEO was exasperated with the rising inventory levels of the pharmacy department. He was frustrated as this was not the first time since the issue had been flagged. Yet, the rise had not been arrested and instead had risen again. He had lost confidence in the current team that was trying to handle the issue. He then extended an open invitation to the room. He asked if anyone else could take up the responsibility to decrease the inventory levels. He also added that if that were not possible, the concerned person would have to submit a detailed report identifying the issues and reasons which have caused the rise. The idea was that the information could aid in addressing these issues.

Perhaps it was because of the nature of the challenge; there was silence. No one volunteered. Then I raised my hand and offered to take up the role. The CEO turned to me and said that my report had to be comprehensive and that I had to provide the real-time analysis and possible steps to address the issues. He also said that it would be an accountable project. I was not deterred.

After that, I spent a few hours every day without neglecting my work as the Medical Administrator to study the inventory issues. My diligence paid off, and I was able to determine the reasons for the rising inventory levels. I had also prepared a set of plans the department could adopt to arrest the rise and bring it down. When I was asked to present my report, I shared my findings and suggestions. I also asked for the CEO's help to communicate with the concerned seniors in the department, lest they think I was over-extending my boundaries.

He agreed, and the pharmacy department implemented my suggestions. By adopting my plan of action, they were able to decrease their inventory levels by 70% within 90 days.

It was a shock to many as this department was in disrepute for its inventory levels. After the 90th day, the process had become standardized. The CEO was very appreciative of me, and he lauded me for taking this accountability project and delivering the required results. However, the biggest lesson for me was learning how accountability functioned, and it has been a part of my work ethic ever since.

What I learned:

- Accountability helped me to achieve a goal by aligning the thoughts.
- It allowed me to prove my worth.
- It gave me the confidence that I could accomplish any task if done with full ownership and accountability.
- Accountability taught me the basics of a particular assignment, which would be so helpful in my future growth.
- It taught me that there is nothing wrong with asking for help when needed.

As I mentioned earlier, sometimes there is a misconception that responsibility can be a burden. But responsibility can be the panacea that grants you grace and strength. Even when hurdles are looming threateningly over you, you will be able to face them with your shoulders squared, head held high, and eyes firm with resolve. You will find an untapped well of tremendous strength and courage to move forward bravely.

Responsibility shapes and drives your resilience. I can say the above lines as I saw my mother living that life. I witnessed it as a child and then realized it as an adult. She raised us with no appropriate economic support. She did it all single-handedly. As kids, we never realized the magnitude of her contribution to our growth.

## A Mother's Love

But when I turned into an adult and became a husband and a father, I realized the extent of the burden she had carried with such forbearance. She never stumbled and always marched ahead with us children in tow. It was the joint wedding reception of my two younger brothers. The day is still prominent in my memory.

By that time, my elder brother and I were already married. We know that marriage is considered as the marker of settling down as a responsible member of society. So, it was a momentous occasion.

It was a great day, and the entire program was carried out flawlessly. My mother was quiet, but we could see the happiness and contentment on her face. We were not worried about her silence as our mother was usually on the quieter side.

We returned home, tired but happy. Suddenly, my mother collapsed on the bed with an emotional breakdown releasing a torrent of tears. It was a shocking sight. It was as if her inner reservoir of strength had been broken. I will never forget her tears and gasps. We were petrified; my wife and I rushed to find a clinical cause for her distress. However, she remained inconsolable. She kept sobbing even as we surrounded her to provide her with whatever she needed. We did not know what was wrong, so we sat down with her and allowed her the time to calm down a little.

I do not remember how long it took, but she calmed down after a while. Her tears were still unstoppable. But she gathered us five children and hugged us. We hugged her back, giving her all the comfort and love we could. Then after a few minutes, she spoke in a heavy voice, "I had held back my tears from the day your father had left us. Today I am crying the way I wanted to cry on that day. When he left us, I knew I had to hold myself, focus all my energy on you, my children. I could not afford to be sentimentally weak. Today after the reception, I realized that I had done my duty, your father had left me with: the responsibility to take care of you.

Now all of you are married, settled in your careers, and I feel I have fulfilled my responsibility. Now I can grieve the loss of my husband with the relief that my sadness will no longer compromise your future." We hugged her. Our mother fulfilled her responsibilities and, for that moment, wanted to be the widow who had to mourn her husband. There is no better example than those impactful lines to explain how responsibility can provide you the inner strength to combat any challenge.

My mother kept the broken pieces of her heart hidden and controlled her emotions. She held it together because she knew that the loss of the father was more impactful than the loss of the husband. So, she stayed strong for us. When responsibility is infused within you, you will be able to transform your emotional setback into strength. My mother did it and expressed her emotions only after settling us all in life.

If you become responsible, you will find that no pain will dissuade you, no adversity will shake you, and no challenge will weaken you. Learn to be accountable and take up responsibility. The road to success is never easy.

Any path to success is peppered with challenges and pitfalls. A responsible individual will know how to stay put throughout the course without blaming anyone else. Such an individual will try to make the best out of any situation, deal with every difficulty with ease, and come out triumphant.

Is there a difference between being responsible and being accountable? Yes. Ask yourself this question: Are you a responsible person? On some days, or for some tasks, you may answer "YES." At other times and for other tasks, you might not be so sure, be it a small or big job.

A responsible person shows this trait in almost everything he does. Being responsible is an attitude and a habit. Whereas, you may not be accountable always; at times, for some tasks, you act with full ownership due to various reasons, and at times you cannot, for some other reasons. Maybe the right thing to say is that a responsible person will almost always be taking full accountability. In contrast, those who are not inherently responsible may only be functioning or behaving as accountable, occasionally or rarely.

I had once come across this wonderful story: Once upon a time, there were four people named Everybody, Somebody, Anybody, and Nobody. They worked in the same organization.

One day their organization assigned an important task, and Everybody was asked to do it. However, Everybody was sure Somebody would do it. Anybody could have done it, but Nobody did it. Somebody was very upset over it because it was Everybody's job. Everybody had thought Anybody could do it, but Nobody thought that Everybody would not do it. Hence it ended up that Everybody blamed Somebody when Nobody did what Anybody could have done.

While we can remark over the smart wordplay, you cannot help but think that it is true in so many cases today. Do not think that someone else can do it; get it done if it falls within your jurisdiction. Here are some points worth noting from the above story:

- Lack of ownership
- No accountability
- Lack of responsibility
- Blame games and finger-pointing

**Responsibility and Accountability at the Workplace**

When you are involved in such behaviors, it does not behoove well for an organization. The organization will not provide the service it was set for as productivity will lag due to such conduct. Everyone will coast along, hoping someone else will pick up the slack. Such attitudes are not sustainable.

It will come calling one day and leave one with lament and regret. If you show your worth as an accountable leader, you will be an asset for any organization and will always be valued and progress further in your career. When a person is responsible, that person is entrusted with the implementation and completion of greater tasks. If you find yourself in a position of accountability and responsibility, fulfill those obligations. You can do it yourself or even delegate when and where appropriate. When you deliver the results needed, you will confirm that you are worth your value within your organization.

There may be occasions when you are unwilling to take up responsibility. It may be due to several reasons. Perhaps it could be a thankless task or an incommodious client who could drive you to the limits of your patience. All these may seem valid reasons for avoiding accountability as a short-term relief; however, they come with a long-term cost.

I am sure you have heard of this proverb: *When the going (circumstances) gets tough, the tough get going.* So, when you neglect responsibility when the situations appear difficult, why should anyone trust you with better opportunities? There is no such thing as fair-weather responsibility. Your mettle is tested during tough and challenging times. You stand to learn from that pressure. Even if you fail, there are lessons to be discovered. You may find out where your deficiencies lie. Perhaps your communication skills need some work, or it could be your delegation.

You will always find areas that need improvement. When you avoid responsibility in tough situations, the shortcomings are marked. When you prevent your chances, you are robbing yourself of a great opportunity to learn. Thus, in the future, when you come across a similar situation and this time if you cannot avoid it, what will you do?

It would be best for you to remember that organizations judge a candidate on attitude through some of the basic exhibitions of responsibility, including how a person takes care of himself and his basic needs, and his family, friends, and colleagues. Responsibility is a key attribute and attitude required for anyone who wants to be successful in life. This is such an important attitude that it makes a difference in how you view yourself and others.

Responsibility empowers you to be accountable for your behavior, think critically, perform ably under any stress or during challenging times, and handle big and small tasks flawlessly with added value.

There are many benefits you can reap by being responsible:

1. **You build strong, lasting relationships.** When you take responsibility for your actions, you will be able to reap the benefits of strong, lasting relationships with your family, friends, and colleagues. Just recall your favorite teachers in life. You will recognize them fondly not because they were lenient toward you. You remember them because they took their responsibility of educating you seriously and treated it with the highest regard. Thus, responsibility is also at the root of building strong, reliable relationships. When you cultivate responsibility within the bonds of a relationship, you will value it more.

You will never have a misplaced sense of ego of not accepting a mistake committed, as you will know that no one is perfect. And that is how you will remain accountable for your day-to-day actions, which in turn fosters trust. This trust creates the foundation for strong, lasting relationships.

2. **You showcase empathy.** A responsible person cares about others and can place themself in the other person's shoes to understand their perspective and act accordingly. A responsible person is taken as a reliable shoulder to lean upon and a helping hand by others when they require it.

3. **You do not blame others.** When you are a responsible leader, you get rid of the habit of blaming others for any problems that arise. That is because a responsible person knows that there is no winner in blame games. And those who are responsible will always focus on finding solutions rather than condemn during adversity. Alyson Noel in his novel *Fated* says *"There is an old and very wise Native American saying: Every time you point a finger in scorn—there are three remaining fingers pointing right back at you."*
\#

4. **You do not become a complainer.** A complainer spreads negativity all over; when you practice responsibility, you will never become a complainer as you will understand that life can be tough at times. You will know that it is better to focus on the silver linings and work to alleviate the situation during such times.

5. **You identify circumstances that can be out of one's control.** If you are a responsible person, you will develop an inherent understanding of when a situation can get out of hand. You will remain calm and composed even in the face of the toughest conditions. You will not shy away from asking for help as your focus will be on finding solutions.

6. **You learn to prioritize.** You will get rid of procrastination and make schedules. You will know your priorities and create sub-goals of the big goals to ensure no delay.

A small but to-the-point checklist works well and is exceedingly popular among those who strive to become more responsible. These lists help to stay on track.

7. **You become a dependable leader.** Responsibility is not a right but a privilege. Responsibility is a trait found in leaders, as leaders focus on the greater, long-term result consistently. A responsible leader invariably keeps things simple and maintains good relationships with others. It could be as simple as arriving at appointments on time or staying at work till late to ensure a job is done successfully and within the timeline mentioned. A responsible leader can be counted on to finish any task to the best of their ability.

**Responsible Leadership**

A responsible leader learns to move from being a victim to becoming a victor. So, this brings us to the question of how you can develop yourself as a responsible person and leader.

I have a few tips that you can follow to develop yourself:

1. **Take responsibility – Own your feelings, thoughts, words, actions:** The first step is to take responsibility for the self. It would be best to realize that your thoughts, feelings, words, and activities are a part of your identity. They display who you are to the world.
So, before you even think of external factors, take care of your personality, thought process, character, and attitude. You should take responsibility for yourself and accept that nobody else can make you think, feel, say, or do anything unless you feel the same. You hold the remote for your life. You control what goes on. You cannot blame someone else for having influenced you. It was your choice to be affected.

2. **Take responsibility – Do not indulge in blame games:** It is easy to apportion blame. You can always find an excuse if needed. You can always find a scapegoat.
Just think of how easy it is to get away or escape by blaming others.

You can blame your parents, partners, friends, or colleagues, or the organization, your upbringing, or even the black cat which crossed the path, if you are so inclined. You can always blame someone else for your failures or misfortune. But such an attitude will only foster a victim mindset. A victim mindset will inhibit you from seeking solutions. However, when you stop blaming others and accept responsibility, you make a shift from being a victim to becoming a victor. This is the secret of winners! Hence, instead of blaming others for failure or a difficult situation, ask yourself: Where did I go wrong? What can I learn? How can I find a solution?

3. **Take responsibility – Do not complain:** Complaining is another feature of a negative mindset. When you constantly complain, you send a message to your brain and to others who notice this behavior: you are a victim and you are helpless to do anything about it. Your mind has to be a hub of innovation, energy, and exploration. But when you send such a signal, you would lose even before starting. Therefore, divert your mind away from such a perspective, and instead look for learning opportunities and focus on solutions. That is the way to begin your journey toward successful leadership.

4. **Take responsibility – Do not take anything personally:** This is a vital step. When you accept this thought, you gain tremendous power. Know that you do not have control over how other people respond. You can only have control over how you respond. If there is an issue, do not take it personally. Focus on the subject and not what it could imply. When someone provides you feedback, they are not implicating you in some fault. They are providing you with clarity. Thus, when you face issues plagued with doubts, ask yourself: Is this about me or the problem that is to be met?

5. **Take responsibility – Be happy:** Your happiness is your responsibility, and do not expect it from anyone else. Be it your partner, parent, friend, colleague, boss, or child, nobody is there to make you happy.

Enjoy their company, but it becomes a difficult relationship if you put the burden of your happiness and worth on them. Indulge in things that make you feel happy, be it music, driving, or anything you like.

6. **Take responsibility – Live in the present:** You can gain nothing from reliving the past glories or dreaming about future conquests. The past is history, and the future is still a mystery. You have no control over either. You can neither change the past nor predict the future. The only choice is the present. You can only control what you can do today, at this very moment. Take charge of it. Own it. That is your responsibility for today. So, make the best out of it.

7. **Take responsibility – Your intention:** What did you have for lunch today? Pizza, fast food, or salad? You chose your lunch. That is the power you possess. We can be ignorant of this power when we choose the dress we wear today, but be conscious of it. If you are trying to lose weight, your choice of fast food can be damaging. It shows a lack of intent in trying to lose weight. You may find an excuse that you had to accompany a friend. But the action is still a choice. If you were forced to go, your silence was a choice. Hence, it is important to use your power of options for your positive development instead of your mind's vision. Be mindful of this power, be it in a relationship, in an organization, or in wealth, fitness, learning, etc. When you choose, ask yourself a simple question: Is this moving me toward my goal?

8. **Take responsibility – Be calm, confident:** When you take responsibility for your life, you will be relaxed and confident. You will be assured with a feeling of consciously being in charge of yourself. You will be aware of your choices and how you will respond according to your preference. When you empower yourself, you will find that you will despise the victim mindset and move toward a victor mindset.

9. **Take responsibility – See good in people:** Follow the advice of Walt Whitman who said, "Be curious, not judgmental." Your prejudices will stop you from learning new perspectives. If you are offended by a friend's actions, look for the intentions behind that action. Do not label them based on one move. Labels are restrictive, and they will stop you from exploring the boundlessness of this world.

10. **Take responsibility – Do things without being asked:** It is self-evident. Doing what is required without being asked to do so is the ultimate display of responsibility. This single trait can open many paths to progress and success. Develop this habit from small actions like emptying the dustbin when you see it overflowing.

11. **Take responsibility – Be honest:** Responsibility goes hand-in-hand with honesty. If you have committed a wrong deed, accept it even if you think there were no witnesses. Accept your mistake, and you will find that subsequent worries and guilt will not haunt you. You will no longer concentrate on the present if you keep silent about your mistakes as the past will hold you to ransom.

12. **Take responsibility – Set priorities:** Set your priorities, and take care of your tasks before you partake in any fun or time-wasting activity.
Start by doing what you need to get done first, and then you can relax and have fun afterward.

Why is accountability such an important leadership principle? Here are five very important reasons.

- Accountability builds trust.
- Accountability improves performance.
- Accountability ensures that you do not waste time on distracting activities.
- Accountability promotes ownership.
- Accountability inspires confidence.

I have another tracker to help you become more responsible and accountable.

From the above 12 actionable pointers of "Take responsibility," pick one which you believe is a challenge to you. Write your steps to work on that in the table below. You may need to develop this table for all the 12 steps or any number you want to work on! You must check the progress as mentioned below, till all of them become your habits.

| Find Your Godfather Inside You | Responsibility and Accountability | Write Here |
|---|---|---|
| Learning Exercise | Write down the actionable from "Take Responsibility" list above that you want to work upon: | Steps decided to work on doing this actionable in your day to day living:<br>1.<br><br>2.<br><br>3.<br><br>4.<br><br>5.<br><br>6. |
| | Practice the decided steps every day, in the following manner | |
| | Follow-up check for practice thrice daily for 10 days – morning, afternoon, night | |

| | Follow-up check for practice twice daily for 10 days – morning, night | |
| --- | --- | --- |
| | Follow-up check for practice once daily for 10 days, at night | |

# 8
# PASSION
Chasing passions and not pensions, keeping the positive fire ignited

*"You have to be burning with an idea, or a problem, or a wrong that you want to right. If you're not passionate enough from the start, you'll never stick it out."* — Steve Jobs

## A Brother's Legacy

My elder brother had just cleared his 12th standard exams and he was discussing his plans for the future. We expected him to pursue some reputed professional degree. But he stunned us all. He said that he wanted to be a businessman. It was a revolutionary choice because none of our family members across generations had ever been businessmen and the trend was to opt for salaried jobs. We expected our father to teach him the error of his thoughts and lead him onto the same path trod by our family for generations.

However, my brother was quite enthusiastic about his ambitions. He discussed the issue with our father for a while. My father was persuaded by his conviction and desire. My elder brother had proposed that he would complete a simple undergraduate course and then set his sights on starting a business. But my father intervened and insisted that he should pursue a professional course of study. His professional degree would help him establish credibility when he started his business.

My father was determined to help him and my brother was emboldened by such strong support. He decided to pursue a degree in engineering, and in fact, did obtain admission to an engineering college to pursue his BE degree. He wanted to use this engineering background to launch his business. He had it mapped out and was sure of his path.

However, as I mentioned previously, we met with a tragedy soon. Our father passed away when he was still in his first year of engineering. When my brother started college, it seemed like he went with stars in his eyes. But on that fateful day, they were clouded with sadness. We knew the reality of our situation. Our financial condition and other related aspects meant that we were going to struggle. Our mother had to take care of him, me, and my two younger brothers. It was a daunting prospect.

But he returned to his college to finish his studies. Many relatives and friends stepped up to help us in a variety of ways. Our maternal uncle helped us by providing a roof over our heads. Others helped by giving us money to survive. So, my brother continued on his path. He passed out with flying colors when he graduated with his degree. Now it seemed as if the weight of the world rested on his shoulders. He was the oldest male member of the family and people expected him to start contributing to our sustenance. He had to start earning to support the family. We assumed that he had forgotten the dream to be a businessman as our circumstances had changed.

We could not be farther from the truth. He had not forgotten his dream. He did not want to toil in the rigors of a job. He wanted to start his business. He wanted to pursue his childhood passion of being an entrepreneur. When he made us aware that he was still going to pursue this dream, we were surprised. We knew that we did not have the financial capital to back him up and none of us had any experience to even support or guide him through this perilous path. It was once again my mother who stepped up for us. She reinforced her confidence in him and his dream. She asked him to pursue it and make it successful. My brother needed no stronger support. He was determined to realize his dream and had the gumption to make his passion come true. Our mother's support was the greatest motivation for him. However, he did not want to forget his responsibilities toward our family. He said that he wanted to consolidate his foundations first. A fair had come to town and would remain for a month.

When such fairs came to town, there used to be temporary job openings for the locals to help in running the tents and stalls at the fair. My brother wanted to find a job at that fair. He had a two-pronged reason. Primarily, he would get firsthand experience in how sales are done and the strategies involved in a business with his daily interactions with the customers and businessmen. Secondly, there would be an inflow of money, however small, into the family. Another allied benefit was that the job was a temporary one and after a month, he could start his business. He got a job in an electronics showroom as a salesman. I remember him returning every night and writing down copious notes on what he had learned that day. He was focused on how you could influence the customer's psyche and how businessmen functioned and drove their businesses.

When he reached the end of his tenure, he realized that he had to learn some more. So, he joined another company that had the same job profile. However, in this new job, there was the added dimension of traveling. He took it up to further his learning. He continued exploring many such opportunities. In every venture, he sought to understand the many nuances and details of running a business. He did not care about the job profile or the industry profile. He took up jobs that could afford him learning opportunities. He worked as an over-the-counter salesman when he could have taken a cushy job with great benefits as a qualified engineer.

I will not forget his face whenever he returned home. The exhaustion was clear, but he seemed happy. He never failed in writing down his notes. It did not matter if he was tired. He would still read the business section of the newspaper. He cut out relevant articles that could help him and always reread his notes. It was clear that he was driven by his passion to be a businessman and every action was geared toward it.

Even as we watched him do these activities, none of us could provide him any input. These activities were all foreign to us. All we knew was that he was striving hard to realize his dream. He was driven and passionate. We knew that even if he had to crawl and inch his way to success, he would do it. However, we had no idea how we could help him. He was an inspiration to himself. There were occasions when we could palpably feel his exhaustion, but he was never demotivated. He had the simmering desire underneath to succeed and never questioned his path.

He was sure of it and blazed ahead with confidence. He was determined to know all the basics of running a business. When he was confident that he had enough knowledge, he approached our brother-in-law. Our brother-in-law was an entrepreneur in Lucknow. My elder brother wanted to consult him and lean on his experience to certify his learnings and understandings. He shared his ideas and thoughts and our brother-in-law was impressed.

He gave him the confidence that he could be successful in business. He also pledged his support at the back end of his operations. This was the vote of confidence that my brother needed. His words and pledge of support instilled tremendous confidence in my brother and our mother. The rest of us now knew that my brother would work unceasingly to realize his long-standing, passionate dream, which he once shared with our father. My brother then worked hard. He was driven by his passion and was ably supported and guided by our brother-in-law. I can say with great pride today that he has been able to create a name for his company and make it a reputable brand. He is one of the renowned and well-respected names in his industry today. Recently, he was rewarded for his vision and his brand was recognized by the most prestigious Indian Industries Association, which elected him unanimously as its Vice President, a designation that is only assigned to the best businessmen in the industry. My brother showed me the value of having a dream and chasing it relentlessly. There were many occasions when he could have given up his efforts and lamented the difficulties. There were occasions when he could have procrastinated and been lethargic for a day. None of us would have begrudged him for taking a day off. But my brother did none of those things. He persevered through the tough times. He found warmth in the fire of his passionate dream even as the cold world outside tried to douse it. He kept going and demanded the best from himself. He lived in his passion, every day. It is this passion, which he nurtured through his devotion and hard work, that enabled him to establish his company as a brand to be reckoned with in his industry. If you were to look at some of the great examples in history, you will find they were driven by passion. Steve Jobs talked of how you should do what you love. Chris Gardner, whose life was the inspiration for the Hollywood film 'The Pursuit of Happyness', talks of how success can be obtained if you *"find something you love to do so much you can't wait for the sun to rise to do it all over again."*

Look at the greatest sportsmen and women and actors and actresses. They were all driven by their passion to be the best at what they did. They dedicated their lives to it. You also have incredible tyros who would have blazed bright and faded away as they were distracted by other trappings of fame. They were never truly passionate about their ambitions, for if they had been so, we would have remembered them as virtuosos and not as what-ifs.

**The Legacy of a Lady Doctor**

I do not need to impress on you the difficulty of doing a specialization in medical subjects. Doing a specialization in any subject is hard. It is extremely challenging in the medical field as it can drain you. You have to put in a tremendous quantity of hours and expend a great deal of energy daily. It can be even more exhausting when you consider the number of patients that one has to treat in a government hospital that is associated with a medical college. But this is also the fruition of one's medical education. A person can withstand this stress only because they would have undergone a far harsher routine when they had to prepare for the postgraduate (PG) course entrance examinations. That is a far more hectic and draining period. There is also a lot of uncertainty during this stage. You need to have a thorough knowledge of all the subjects as the questions are multiple-choice questions. It means you need to know a lot more than for a subjective essay-based examination. There is no scope for half marks. You either get it right or you do not. It was even harder during my time as we did not have a common exam such as NEET. There were only a few colleges that conducted these entrance exams. You then had to contend with a large number of applicants who would have studied as hard as you. Then there were the various quotas, which would also reduce the number of seats available to students.

It was during this time that a lady doctor who had just finished her MBBS course tried to clear the PG entrance examination. She was clear in her ambition to have a specialization in her chosen field. She had gotten married much earlier.

Her first attempt was further complicated when she realized that she was pregnant. However, she attempted the examination after taking all the due considerations. She failed to clear the exam. A failure of that nature could have demoralized many, but not her.

She was truly passionate about her field and wanted to have a specialization in it. You may have the misconception that passion gives you boundless energy: it does not. Everyone is prone to have weaker and discouraging moments. Everyone needs a slight push and motivation to come back re-energized. The woman in the story, after delivering her first child, was exhausted. She doubted if she should continue pursuing her passion for a PG degree or go back to the workforce. It was just a moment of weakness. She even approached her husband for his input. Her husband reminded her of her passion and asked her to study for the entrance examination. If she took up a job, she would have to kiss the dream of a PG degree goodbye as she would never have the time to study. The lady found solace in his words and returned to her task with renewed zeal and energy.

There were times when even as she fed the baby, she would be reading from the textbooks. There were occasions when the husband found her asleep out of exhaustion with an open book and a sleeping baby on her lap. She was taking care of the baby and the house, and also preparing for one of the toughest exams in the world at that point. Lesser minds would have cracked under the pressure. But she did not complain even once. She was able to take care of the child and the home, and yet find hours in the day for her studying. She bobbed her way through the stormy waves as steadily as she could. She did all these tasks with focus and undying passion.

She passed the exam on her second attempt. Later she would also get her specialization in her chosen field. Her dream had come true. Why? She was passionate about her dream and worked on it to make it happen. The seed which germinated her success was her passion.

I can attest to this story. I witnessed her moments of struggle, the moments that seemingly defeated her desire. I saw her unbreakable desire come to the fore. I saw her success and I was there for all of them. She is my wife and life partner.

I can give personal testimony for my wife as I saw her passionately fight against all odds. She faced the most incredibly challenging circumstances. Yet she was nothing but a wonderful demonstration of grace and passion.

> *"If you feel like there's something out there that you're supposed to be doing, if you have a passion for it, then stop wishing and just do it."* — Wanda Skyes

## Passions Persevered

Passion can help shape the direction of your life. It can make you challenge the notion of predestined fate. You need look no further than the Jamaican bobsleigh team in the Winter Olympics of 1988. Four men participated in the event as newcomers. None of them had ever participated in a bobsleigh tournament prior to the Olympics. However, they did want to represent Jamaica at the Olympics. The bobsleigh tournament is an event that relies on the sprinting skills of its contestants. They had the basic ingredients for the event but for one crucial element. Jamaica is a tropical island and the bobsleigh is a team sport wherein four contestants make timed runs on narrow, banked, twisting iced tracks. They practiced in Jamaica without the icy mountains and got a chance to participate in the qualifiers and qualified for the Olympics with one teammate getting injured in the process. The brother of another teammate who had flown in to show his support took the injured contestant's place. They never won a medal in the event. But in one of the more iconic Olympic moments, they won a lot of hearts when they picked up their overturned and broken bobsled and walked across the finish line.

Three of the contestants would return in 1992 and 1994. In 1994, they would finish 14th, ahead of the more fancied teams from Russia, Australia, France, and the United States of America. The Jamaican bobsleigh team would return to the Winter Olympics in 1998, 2002, and 2014, and a women's team would debut in 2018. That was the legacy of the original team. Their passion to represent their country at the Olympics, even in an event so foreign to them, would inspire future generations to repeat their feat.

Passion can change your fate. However, it depends on what passion you nurture. If you have a positive passion like becoming a successful and influential leader, you will become one. On the other hand, if you have a negative passion to become a nefarious criminal, you will find yourself willfully breaking laws to become one. Think of passion as what carves the path for you to travel on.

It can hew the brambles of doubts and soothe the bruises and blisters on your feet when you tread on rocky grounds. I recall a colleague, whom I had met immediately after completing my MBBS course. I had just started my ad-hoc housemanship in a government hospital in Delhi. His name was Nilanjan.

He, too, like me had joined the hospital after his MBBS course. He came from a small town near Kolkata and had completed his MBBS course in one of the government medical colleges in Kolkata. I remember him clearly; he was quite ordinary looking and dark-complexioned like most Indians.

There was nothing about him physically that could make him stand out from the crowd unless it was his poor understanding of Hindi. However, he stood out for me due to his extraordinary ambitions. I had joined a week earlier, and thus, I was entrusted with the responsibility of introducing him to everyone in the department and giving him a tour of the premises.

I knew immediately that he was going to be someone great. As we introduced ourselves, I could see that he struggled with the Hindi language. I was curious and asked him why he came to Delhi when there were numerous hospitals in Kolkata. Why would he give himself a handicap when he was not fluent in Hindi and come to Delhi? He was candid in his reply. He told me that he came from a very poor family. However, they had somehow managed to fund his MBBS course. He knew the reality of his situation and wanted to live up to his family's faith in him and pay back his gratitude. His aim was to move to the United Kingdom (UK) to work. He could then justify the investment of faith made by his family. He would also then be able to provide them with better living conditions based on that salary. He was determined to clear the PLAB examination, which is essential for a doctor to practice in the UK. However, this was not a pipe dream. The exam would be held in the UK. He knew that the exam fee, travel, and accommodation would be very expensive. He was determined to fund himself for this venture. So, he came to Delhi where he would have a higher remuneration. The stipend in Delhi was three times what he would have received in Kolkata. He had estimated that he would be able to save a lot more money in Delhi.

The plan was to save money until he hit a particular mark and then he would take the exam in the UK. He was also confident that he would be able to study for the exam in the intervening years.

He also had the innate confidence that he could pass the exam. Even as he let me in on his plans, I could see the vigor in his eyes. There was an honesty in them. I could feel his deep-rooted passion to achieve these goals for the betterment of his family. I could not help but feel impressed and inspired by him.

I remember my initial days of working with him. We worked closely together and had become good friends. He used to rely on my help to navigate city life in Delhi. In the early days, I had to hold his hand and help him cross the wide roads that were chock-a-block with traffic. He was scared of the big city.

I remembered his dream, and whenever we were together, I did my best to contribute toward it. I paid all the expenses so that he could add that additional amount of money to his savings, thereby bringing his goal of going to the UK that much closer. A few months later, I got the chance to join AIIMS and I took it.

Nilanjan stayed back in the same hospital. However, I used to go back often to meet him as he was a good friend. Then he got an opportunity to do his housemanship in another hospital in Delhi. I felt that he slipped away from me when he went to that hospital. So, whenever we met, I used to remind him of his passion and his dream. I tried to make him recall that Kolkata boy who had come to Delhi to achieve his dreams.

I tried every method in the book. I spoke to him, reminded him, and even cajoled him to save money. I wanted him to remember his dream to practice in the UK. However, I noticed that he was not so passionate about that dream anymore. His carefree attitude gnawed at me and I could sense that something was wrong. I wanted to find out what was happening.

However, I could also sense that our relationship did not have the same intimacy as before. He seemed more withdrawn and I did not want to fray our relationship any further by being inquisitive.

I found the answer to my doubts a few months later. I went to his place to meet him one evening. I knew that he was off-duty that evening. However, he was not in his room. However, I met his roommate, who had also become a close acquaintance of mine. I asked him when I could expect to see Nilanjan. He told me not to bother as he would only return at midnight or worse, the next morning.

I had a faint sense of foreboding. But I pushed my thoughts aside and asked him if Nilanjan was on night duty. I could feel my stomach drop when I heard him answer in the negative. His roommate told me that Nilanjan had bought a bike and my stomach dropped further when I heard this.

I was wondering how a man who was saving money to go to the UK could decide to buy a bike. It stunned me.

His roommate, however, provided me with the missing information to complete the picture by revealing a few more shocking facts. It is one of the oldest and well-known stories. Nilanjan had strayed down the path of temptations and was now hanging around with the wrong crowd. His roommate told me how he roamed around on his off-duty days with these people. They would drink alcohol and party around like they had no cares.

He used to only return late in the night or early in the morning. He would return completely inebriated, smelling of cigarettes and alcohol. I was astonished by these stories. I could not help but recall the distance I had been feeling between us and the sense of foreboding that had been in my mind. I remembered now how he used to brush me off whenever I tried to remind him of his dreams.

I met him a few more times after that day. I confronted him and asked him why he had changed. I could see that he was indifferent to my questions and he gradually started to avoid me. The last time I met him, he became angry with me for questioning him. He told me that he had chosen to lead his life this way now.

He was living it the way he wanted, with fun and partying; he wanted to be like his new friends. He had lost his passion and despite my many efforts to remind him of it, he was not bothered anymore. I had no choice but to leave him to his own devices.

My interactions with Nilanjan taught me many things:

- Passion can be positive; passion can be negative
- Positive passion will give you the strength to inch closer to your long-term goal
- Negative passion will make you weak with regard to your positive passion, and divert your energy toward the negative goals
- If you are a weak person, there will be enough hindrances to deter you from your goal by enticing you with short-term gains
- Following your passion is a test of your character
- Success comes to you when you follow your passion without falling prey to the distractions
- Following your passion is a daily activity and commitment

## As Much as You Want to Breathe

There is a famous story of a young man who once approached Socrates, the Greek Philosopher. The young man was not known for being overly passionate about any goals in life. However, he asked Socrates, "I want to have knowledge." Socrates was not convinced with his manner of asking and did not see any passion in his request. So, he took the young man down to the sea.

Socrates then dipped the young man's head and held it under the water for thirty seconds. When he loosened his hold, the young man came out sputtering. Socrates asked him to repeat what he wanted. He replied, "I want knowledge." It was as if Socrates was enraged by his answer. He pushed his head under the water once again.

This time he held him underwater for longer than thirty seconds. Even when the young man thrashed about trying to come up for air, Socrates held him still. Then he suddenly let go of him. The young man came out of the water gasping. Socrates then asked him to repeat once more what he wanted. The young man let out a gasp, "Air, I want air!" Then Socrates replied, "That is what I wanted to teach you. When you thirst for knowledge as much as you did for air right now, you will do anything to have it."

This is a classic example of understanding what passion means, and it shows that if you desire something badly, you will find the ways and means and the willpower to achieve it. The only way to convert that desire into reality is to develop a passion for it. And if you have the passion, any desire will turn into a reality.

An interesting study conducted in Nigeria showed that more than 50 percent of all CEOs in Nigeria had obtained a 'C' or lower grade average in their higher education. Nearly 80 percent of all Nigerian Presidents were in the lower half of the merit ranking in their school classes. It also showed that more than 65 percent of all millionaire entrepreneurs either never attended a higher educational institution or were dropouts.

In light of these findings, this is the question that comes to our minds: What made these seemingly ordinary people achieve extraordinary things in life? The answer lies in one word, passion. It is their passion and their commitment to it that differentiates these successful leaders from the rest.

## Metamorphosing Dreams into Reality

It is their passion that separated them from the common folk and it is their commitment to that passion that separated them from the dreamers. Their passion ensured they continued to succeed in their lives. If they had not possessed that passion, these people would have been as ordinary as anyone else.

These winners realized much early in their lives that to achieve anything, passion must come first. Think of great leaders, and you will be struck by their passion: Zik for One Nigeria, Gandhi for human rights, Churchill for freedom, Martin Luther King Jr. for equality, Bill Gates for technology, Mother Teresa for service to the poor, Robert W. Woodruff for coke at every table, etc. The lives of these men and women went beyond the ordinary, and they had the great desire to change the world as they saw it.

They had the passion, commitment, and conviction. Powerful leaders have these qualities in large measures. They also insist on sharing it, constantly.

Their passion is not directionless. It is sharply focused on what they want to achieve. It is concentrated, and, like a laser beam, it cuts through objections, obstacles, and negativity. It is hard to say no to someone who cares so strongly about something; we find ourselves being unable to resist being drawn into their vision and becoming engaged.

It is passion that causes people to stay up late and get up early. It is passion that helps relationships flourish. Passion gives your life power, energy, and meaning. Greatness cannot be achieved without the passion to become great, be it the aspiration of an athlete, an artist, a scientist, a parent, or a businessman. Whenever anything fires our soul, impossibilities vanish. So, never underrate the power of passion.

Passion is an important key to success. In fact, if you observe successful leaders closely, you will realize they are typically very passionate about their jobs. They, more or less, think, act, and live out their passion day in and day out. They not only work for long hours, but also invariably their passion is on their mind when they go to sleep and when they wake up as well. That is what passion does to you; it makes you fall in love with what you do. This is why I say passion is a key to success. Here are a few reasons why passion is vital to your success:

1. **Passion stops you from giving up:** When you have passion deep down toward a task, you will stop caring about the results. Hence, you will not entertain thoughts of giving up. If you are passionate about helping others, it would not matter to you if there is no one to witness when you help a blind person cross the road. You will continue to be caring toward others, even if no one is aware that you have such a compassionate nature.

2. **Passion pushes you to work harder:** When you have a passion for something, you do not count the hours taken for executing that task. You become involved and obsessed with your work. You do not realize the passage of time. You will enjoy your work so much that the time spent on that work becomes a productive hour.
Passion toward your work keeps you from indulging in meaningless activities and wasting time. In the truest sense, when you have passion, your work becomes your worship.

3. **Passion changes your attitude:** Passion makes you a positive person. You will see opportunities where others may spy a difficulty. People who are not passionate about their work, tend to have a negative attitude during tough times and will exhibit a victim mindset.

4. **Passion makes you motivated:** Passion ensures that you remain inherently motivated toward your work. When you are in this motivated frame of mind you will be able to access an inexhaustible source of energy. You feel an undying responsibility toward your work and its completion, with added value.

5. **Passion drives loyalty:** Passion invariably makes you honest and loyal toward your work, because the desire for this work originates from deep within you. No one has to tell you what to do, as you will be loyal toward your task. You will look to improve and enhance your skill and productivity even if there are no witnesses to see you do it. You will do it simply because you want to be better at it.

6. **Passion makes you focused:** Passion creates a positive cycle—you become obsessed with your work, and you would do anything to acquire more knowledge. This desire helps you sharpen your focus. Focus stops you from wasting time. You will look to be more productive, and this leads to success.

So, how do you know whether you are passionate toward your task or goal? There can be many tests, but you can find the answer through a simple question. Just ask yourself, "Will you do what you are doing, free of cost, without any appreciation, and without any scope for promotion? If your answer is yes, then you surely have the passion, and you will reach great heights of success in your career, sooner or later. However, if you find yourself appalled by the notion of doing the said work for free, it is because you have the wrong ideas behind your work. You are being driven by money, applause, and promotion. You are not truly passionate about your work. You will never find internal happiness and will only subject yourself to severe stress even as you ascend the corporate ladder. Hence, passion is important not only for your success, but also for you to remain stress-free, happy, and contented.

Now, some of you may discover that you are not passionate about your work. You may be feeling lost, especially if you are working long hours at your job. You may be wondering if there is anything you could do to remedy the situation. I can offer you hope. It is never too late. You can still become passionate about your work if you truly want to. Passion is not reflected in your age. Passion is reflected in your will and desire. If you are reading these lines, know that you have already taken the first step to becoming passionate. Follow these steps and you will find your passion that you can chase.

**Finding Your Passion**

The first step is to **Identify Your Passion**. The best way to find your passion is to evaluate what you are already doing. If your current job or work makes you happy, contented, and satisfied with your accomplishments, then you are already following your passion! If you do not realize the aforementioned feelings from your job, then it is time to make a list. List all the activities that make you happy. It could be a hobby or a work activity.

Let us say one of the responsibilities in your job profile is to train newcomers or speak at public forums, and you enjoy these tasks more than your other responsibilities. Then your core job is not your passion. Your passion lies in another area such as being a trainer, speaker, or teacher.

The second step is to **Develop Your Passion.** Once you have found or recognized your passion, then work for it. Elaborating on the previous example, if your passion lies in being a trainer or speaker, then work on becoming a trainer or a speaker. What is it that you have to do? What is it that you can do in the market today? How can you become the best at it? What knowledge should you gather and how should you gather it? Are there any courses or certifications that can help you? Thus, work on developing your passion so that you can work on it as a professional.

The third step is to **Set Small Tasks**. It is important to break your goal down into small goals. If you want to be a speaker, it can be quite intimidating to change your career, especially if you have been entrenched in it for several years. There could be doubts about job or financial stability and you would keep second-guessing yourself. After all, they say that a bird in hand is worth more than two in the bush. Hence, it is important to break down your ambitions into small manageable milestones. If you want to be a speaker, you could start by seeking more speaking engagements at your current job. You could also enroll in some skill-enhancing courses.

You can apply for a few certifications that may come in handy in your quest for a new position. So, plan out these preliminary preparations and make a timeline for their completion. Ensure to keep it manageable. Do not overwhelm yourself all at once. Be patient, but march forward with a plan and with certainty. Work on how you can make your passion your profession. You can simultaneously take other steps such as creating a strong, professional profile or website to spread the word to your contacts, etc.

The **fourth** step is to **Find Accountability**. It is not enough to just create your sub-goals. It is also essential that you have an accountability system for your milestones. The accountability lies with you. And you can decide what reminder system you wish to use to help you live up to your self-assigned accountability. You can also look to a family member or a close friend to be your accountability partner to remind you of your goals.

However, your success will be more assured and quicker, if you look to your innermost Godfather to be your accountability partner. You are the best person to remind yourself about your self-assigned accountability for your sub-goals. When you become your own accountability partner, you need not depend on anyone else for your success.

The fifth step is to **Re-evaluate Your Progress**. It is very important to monitor your progress. Hence, you must evaluate your progress on the decided timeline to see how you are moving toward your goal.

Frequent re-evaluation of your progress enables you to make changes in your plans or sub-goals, sooner rather than later, should you wish to do so.

These aforementioned five steps will not only help you find your passion, but also show you how you can work on it. Finding your passion will have the following effects:

- Help you in your creativity and innovation
- Make you more focused
- Make you continually work on excellence
- Keep you high on energy
- Ensure you contribute more
- Keep you more motivated
- Give you more satisfaction

- Ensure you remain stress-free; your work will not be a burden to you
- Teach you to prioritize
- Teach you the importance of time-management
- Ignite your fire to be an achiever
- Make you enjoy your work
- Help you challenge yourself to better your own performance
- Build a positive attitude toward your work

Use the five steps and the following table to find your passion and be the tracker for your accountability.

| Find Your Godfather Inside You | Passion | Write Here |
|---|---|---|
| Learning Exercise | Identify your passion (anything that you enjoy doing, as your goal of passion): | Sub-goals you have decided on; practice doing these tasks daily, with accountability:<br>1.<br>2.<br>3.<br>4.<br>5. |
| | | **Your accountability partner:** |
| | Check on the decided sub-goals every day, in the following manner | |
| | Follow-up check for practice thrice daily for 10 days – morning, afternoon, night | |
| | Follow-up check for practice twice daily for 10 days – morning, night | |

|  | Follow-up check for practice once daily for 10 days, at night | |

# 9
# EYE FOR DETAIL
Finding magic in the details, and knowing the difference between mediocrity and excellence

*"It's attention to detail that makes the difference between average and stunning."* – Francis Atterbury

**The CEO's Visit**

I have shared the story of how I moved into hospital management in an earlier chapter. Once I had moved into it and oriented myself to the job profile, I realized that I had a knack for it. It was not just that I was good at it, but I enjoyed it too. I have always had the ambition to lead an entire organization.

I wanted to be the captain of the ship. So, I took up roles that would teach me something new every time. All the action plans that I have drawn up in the previous chapters are the fruits of my experience. I used to toss in bed at night, wondering what I was missing to become a leader. I wrote down my goals and sub-goals, made timelines, and followed up on everything I could. I took up a post-graduate course to learn and add more credibility to my profile. I read the latest books and research papers to further my knowledge. I did it all without letting it hamper my work. Over time, I acquired the knowledge and also honed the traits and skills required for the job. I learned about the organizational hierarchy and to identify the line between taking the initiative and trespassing.

However, I continued to feel that I was missing something. I was constantly updating and upgrading my knowledge and skill. But I could not negotiate some matters as efficiently as I hoped to; sometimes, I faltered at a basic level. I wanted to identify the missing element.

One day, I got the opportunity to accompany my CEO on a visit to a facility to check on its upkeep. I held a senior position within the hierarchy, and I did not need to go on such visits. But I went as I wanted to see the CEO in action. I wanted to know where the chasm lay in my learning. I tried to quench the burning fire that kept reminding me that I was missing some key ingredient.

As we went around the premises, I could see that it was very well maintained. The place appeared clean and the materials on the tables were well organized; I could see that there was order within the area. It was not a surprise to me as I was part of the team that conducted ward rounds in these wards twice daily. The place was spic-and-span as usual. However, I learned where the CEO differed from me. I was used to giving cursory looks and taking matters at their face value. The CEO was meticulous. He took his time inspecting every single element. I realized that day that I only beheld stuff with my naked eyes. Numerous details prop up the exterior, but the devil lies in the details, no matter how godly the surface appears.

When I had visited the premises an hour earlier, I had found the place orderly and clean. But the CEO was not satisfied. On that day, he demonstrated how one could check if something was up to the mark. It was an eye-opening experience, which began as soon as he entered the ward. I had walked through the same doors countless times, but I was surprised when he stopped immediately. The areas near the door and the door per se seemed clean. However, as he held the door and swung it to and fro a few times, we heard the door creak from its hinges. Then he shifted a few tables to the side, and we could see that the floor was dirty as the area beneath the tables had not been cleaned.

In another room, he opened a cupboard. The clothes and files were so haphazardly stored that they almost fell on his head. The cabinet was a complete contrast to the orderliness in the room. The items stored in the cupboard were disorganized, and it seemed like everything had been dumped inside to keep it hidden. He found many such tiny flaws. These may seem minor, but in a hospital, they can turn into a far more serious problem.

As he was leaving, he stopped by the notice board, and I saw the problem with it as well. It featured roster shifts and notices that were over a month old. The notice board had many such notices that were not needed.

After spending almost an hour with him, we witnessed shocking revelations. Like a hurricane had made landfall, we could see the disorderliness of the hospital. When he finished his tour, he called all of us into a room. He explained each flaw and how it could adversely affect the hospital. I could see that he was disappointed. He indicated that there were three reasons for this level of negligence:

- There was a lack of basic knowledge on how to take care of these details.
- There was a lack of willingness to do these seemingly minor things.
- The eye for detail, which was missing.

The phrase, Eye for detail, was not new to me, but I received a live demonstration of it in practice on that day. I had never imagined the relevance of this term. The CEO showed me what I lacked. I had been so busy trying to fill in the gaps in my knowledge that I was unaware of the depth that I needed. In my pursuit of knowledge, I had only given a hurried glance for understanding how each department functioned.

I was only looking at the width of knowledge that my mind was missing. So, I was quick to learn the processes and functioning of these departments. The obvious drawback of this approach was that I only knew the broader picture. I had no real understanding of what was present underneath.

I did not look to understand why a particular process was chosen. What were the sub-steps included within one aspect of the process? Which parts needed upgrading? What are the steps that need to be taken to maintain the functions? What would happen if one action was taken wrongly or missed? These were the details and depth I had neglected to investigate. It was then I realized that the void I had felt was not the lack of breadth of knowledge, but the fact that I had no eye for detail, while acquiring the knowledge about other processes, departments, and verticals. That one trip with the CEO enlightened me of the things that were not part of any curriculum.

## The Importance of Having an Eye for Detail

Having an eye for detail is a fundamental skill that is needed to succeed. This skill is more of an art than science. It would help if you learned which details are of importance and which are less so.

You need this skill to understand and improve the effectiveness, efficiency, comprehension, and functioning of processes and systems. The aim is to reduce the number and chances of errors. If you wish to be an effective, transformative, and successful leader, you need an eye for detail to deliver quality work. However, I do not think that having an eye for detail is the only requirement to become a leader. It is a basic necessity for any worker in any role. As I mentioned, the aim is to reduce the margin for error. So, anyone who contributes to an organization will need to follow those aims and produce quality work. It translates across to personal lives as well. It would be best if you connected with the people around you. What do successful organizations have in common? They have employees at relevant positions and roles with an excellent eye for detail. With this skill, the companies are at minimal risk for errors and thus save enormous time on checks, cross-checks, revisions, re-dos, etc.

When you have a good eye for detail, it means you place great importance on thoroughness, accuracy, and consistency in all your tasks.

Assuming you do not have an eye for detail, you will be desultory and be moving forward as a reaction to your circumstances. Your circumstances will control you, and you will not finish your work with any desired level of effectiveness or efficiency. Let us say you have a deadline to meet, and if you do not have a keen eye for detail, you will not plan to finish it. You may instead be rushing to complete it at the last minute. Such work is generally shoddy and careless. When you display that type of productivity, you are also showing an attitude of carelessness.

Another issue could arise in case of emergencies; you will be caught short and create snags within the process. With this kind of productivity, it will be clear that you cannot be trusted to do your work sincerely, let alone with a leadership role. Such workers will require extra supervision with multiple checks and cross-checks by other supervisors and managers who could have contributed better elsewhere. This trait has emerged as one of the most required core competencies for any candidate.

Organizations know that they have to hire people who have this trait to take the initiative and meet challenges. Do not be a drone and think of the next step alone. Cultivate this trait so that you can distinguish yourself as wheat from the chaff. Let me illustrate the importance of a good eye for detail further. Let us say it is the eve of a long weekend.

The Finance Manager of a technology company has made plans to go on a holiday and is in hurry to leave; he has yet to document a few payments which the department would process.

However, one of the suppliers has not yet supplied the invoice to release the amount as per protocol. The payment has to be made by the evening, and the manager does not want to wait any longer. So, he delegates this task to one of the new hires. He reasons that the new hire would be able to do it as the task is primarily a data entry job. He instructs the concerned team member and leaves. The person who was delegated with the task puts in the entry in the required column. It was a bill for Rs 50,000. However, the manager did not warn him that he had to be careful when he made the entry as there would be two columns. The international suppliers were paid in dollars, and the local suppliers were paid in rupees. The new hire also did not check this and just followed the example. He then forwarded the document to another team that processed the payments. The person who processed the payments was also in a hurry. So, he, too, did not check the amounts entered and processed the payment. So, the company, instead of paying Rs 50,000, ended up paying $50,000. The issue would also become serious as the error would not be detected until the completion of the long weekend. So, where did the process break down? We can always apportion the blame; however, the operation failed at every stage.

The manager did not warn the new hire. The new hire did not check the document closely enough, and similarly, the person who processed the payment did not peruse the details. None of the persons concerned had an eye for detail. As illustrated in the example, lack of an eye for detail can lead to a financial loss for the organization and major embarrassment in front of a supplier or a customer. This trait is even more important when it comes to matters like Memorandums of Understanding and other agreements. The lack of an eye for detail could bring forth legal challenges and lawsuits for an organization. Now you know why the idiom 'read the fine print' is so popular.

Having an eye for detail is a necessary skill and a critical performance measuring criterion amongst highly professional employers and companies. It is not valued in just finance or legal departments. It is also a highly valued skill in departments like Administration, Projects Management, Journalism, Marketing, Public Relations, Customer Service, Billing, Quality, Human Resources, etc.

Eye for detail falls under the Big 5 personality traits of conscientiousness as a part of the psychology parameter. Those having this quality, invariably, are also found to be:

- Methodical
- Disciplined
- Meticulous
- Focussed
- Diligent
- Hardworking

There is research that proves a strong, positive correlation between conscientiousness and overall job performance. Conscientiousness enhances the chances of success. At the same time, poor performance is linked to carelessness displayed by people who do not have an eye for detail.

> *"The difference between something good and something great is attention to detail."* – Charles R Swindoll

## A Misplaced Check

A member of any organization needs to have an eye for detail. Its absence will only cause harm and unnecessary confusion. When you lack an eye for detail, sometimes the ensuing errors are spotted only after it is too late. Occasionally, organizations would not even know where to look, in case of a setback resulting from the lack of an eye for detail.

I recall an incident where I saw how a lack of an eye for detail could cause issues. I also realized how this lack of an eye for detail can be contagious and spread across various levels. Such an issue can cause severe problems if not addressed immediately.

It also highlights that the organization does not have a firm grip over its processes. Some years ago, I joined a new organization. I had taken the opportunity to advance my career further. I had a very fruitful month, and I was happy.

At the end of the month, I was having a conversation with my wife. I noticed an incoming notification. Amidst the animated discussion, I just glanced at the message to see if an emergency response was required. It was a message notifying me that my salary had been credited to my bank account. So, I put the phone aside.

We soon switched on the television and started watching a movie. My phone suddenly beeped again to let me know of another notification. I took a glance, and I saw that salary from my previous organization had also been credited to my account. I put the phone aside, perplexed. I presumed it could be a prank or a spam message. However, it gnawed at me that there was something wrong. I could not sit still, and I checked the SMS again. It was there in black and white. I had been paid a salary despite leaving the company over a month ago. I could see that there was a mistake somewhere. I called my bank to find out if such a transaction had indeed occurred. The bank also confirmed that this was the case.

I was confused as I had settled all matters with my previous organization before I left the company. There were no dues that had to be paid to me. So, I called the Head of the Human Resources department of my previous company. I asked him if the company owed me any money. He was surprised, and he said that there were no dues. He asked me for a few minutes to verify the same. I agreed, and the call was disconnected. He called me back after a few minutes and confirmed that there were no dues. He also explained that my account was also closed. I stunned him when I said that I had been credited my salary despite not working for them any longer. I also shared my SMS with him to provide the proof.

I could sense that he had immediately scrambled to sort out the mess. I also received a call from the Head of the Finance Department. He, too, concurred that the transaction was a mistake. He then asked me if I could refund the money using a check. I agreed and asked him to send someone trustworthy to collect the check from him. He immediately consented. I wrote the check and gave it to the concerned person after he had proved his identity. This story has a relatively happy ending. What if the same happened to a disgruntled ex-employee?

Would they come forward with such an admission? I am not trying to cast any aspersions on others, but it is a distinct possibility that someone would keep silent and potentially collect checks to which he is not entitled. When I interacted with my previous organization, I did not need to escalate the matter to the CFO, CHRO, or CEO. If I did broach this issue with any of them, it could have caused ramifications for the team that caused this error. If I were to take this incident in isolation, one team could see it as an error. However, if we were to examine and analyze it carefully, we can see the breakdown in the eye for detail. There were many people involved in this process. This issue can be traced to the mechanical execution of duties without any mindfulness. What does this mean?

- The closure of my account in the previous organization was not done properly, and there was no verification being executed.
- It could also be an error wherein my account was still usable. It could have been made active by the staff completing the transaction and not cross-checking.
- When the salaries for the employees were debited from the company account, no one cross-checked the gross balance in the company's account. Neither the HR nor the Finance departments looked to corroborate the details.
- The salary can only be credited to the employees after cross-checking their attendance records. Since I was no longer with the company, my attendance should have read zero, thus making the salary payable zero as well. There was either a problem with the attendance measurement software or with some particular step in the process.
- More worryingly, if the process itself was so susceptible and porous, it opened up scope for rampant mismanagement and embezzlement.

As listed above, you can see the process fails at various levels due to the lack of an eye for detail across roles and departments. It means that the eye for detail has to be a part of the company's work culture. It is not enough to think that only certain positions need to have an eye for detail, and the others can just be directed. Anyone could have noticed that I had been paid a salary when I no longer worked there.

As I mentioned above, there were many places where this error could have been identified. This culture has to come from the top. People should be discouraged from working casually. The importance of a good eye for detail has to be stressed and taught within the work culture. Do not be fooled into thinking that one person in a critical role can oversee all the issues; recall the previous example where a transaction was approved for $50,000 instead of Rs 50,000. The Finance Manager could have possessed a good eye for detail. But on that day, he was in a hurry and forgot to mention all the details to his colleague. The problem here was that the colleague did as he was directed. If he had had an eye for detail, he would have spotted the issue before making any entry in the document. You have to ensure that this culture is set, and you have to lead by example.

In the case of my previous company paying me a salary after I had left the organization, I was driven by my eye for detail and integrity. I can think of the repercussions in that organization had I not raised the issue and resolved it quickly and amicably.

I can only foresee the troubles if a disgruntled ex-employee refused to acknowledge and return the money. Some people could have been relieved of their jobs, and they could have faced unnecessary legal challenges and hassles.

## Packing Style and Lacking Substance is a No Fly(er)

One of the most influential figures in jazz, Louis Armstrong, once supposedly remarked, *"If I don't practice for a day, I know it. If I don't practice for two days, the critics know it. And if I don't practice for three days, the public knows it."* He could say that because the details would make it clear. Only he who diligently practiced every day would notice that he got a note wrong or the tempo slightly slower immediately. That should be the focus of your eye for detail.

If you have an eye for detail or a lack of it, you will provide impressions of yourself to your peers and seniors that are advantageous or disadvantageous. I remember another incident that I had come across during my career. The story is about how a prospective client was lost because of the lack of a keen eye for detail. I was that prospective customer, and I can show you how that lack of eye for detail gave the wrong impression. One day, in the year 2009, I went to the market to buy some groceries.

As was the norm for me, I parked my car in one of my regular spots. It was convenient as it was near the market and it was also a parking zone. Thus, I never had the fear that it could be towed away by the police. However, there was one drawback to parking at that spot. It was also a spot for people with different flyers. They advertised for gyms, restaurants, and internet service providers, among others. I am sure many of you can imagine a similar scenario.

There would be occasions when I would come to find three to four flyers tucked under my windshield wipers. Some people were creative by somehow affixing it in the gap between the car doors. When I encountered such flyers, my standard operating procedure was to crumple them and throw them away into the nearest garbage bin. On this particular day, I returned to my car and was surprised. It seemed to be a slow day as only one flyer was tucked under the windshield wiper. After I placed the bags inside the car, I returned to the front. I intended to take the paper and crumple it immediately. However, when my fingers touched it, I knew there was something different. This flyer felt premium. It did not have the sensation of a rough paper flyer; this was glossy, and it gleamed. It caught my attention. So, instead of crumpling it, I unfurled the flyer. My eyes were immediately drawn to the color and design of the flyer.

It was bright enough without being garish. I had not seen such a good flyer in my life. I saw that it was advertising a local eatery. It had been inaugurated recently, and my immediate thoughts were that this place would be a success. I was so impressed that I was even considering picking up some food from this seemingly amazing eatery and taking it home. That thought immediately caused a rumble in my stomach. So, I directly scanned the flyer to find the menu and the prices. My attention was first distracted by the prices as they seemed reasonable. I was even more attracted to this restaurant. Then I saw the dishes being sold. The rumblings in my stomach quietened immediately.

The spellings of the dishes were all misspelled. They had the design and the layout so well planned, and overall, it was an excellent flyer. But those spelling mistakes immediately brought the attraction down. I crumpled the paper and threw it in the nearby bin, and went home. On the face of it, this incident might seem rather common and not so surprising. Many of you may have had similar experiences where a single aspect would have served to shift your entire perspective.

It was simply the fact that they did not take care of those small details. Would they have the same lackluster approach to the bigger aspects of their business as well? In my case, I could see the pains they had taken for their advertising. But that one aspect tainted the entire process. I am not trying to make a mountain out of a molehill here.

However, this is how the customers' minds work. You will never know how important these details can be and how adversely they affect you. I remember reading a short story about how one small detail could change someone's life. The story goes thus: A man was on death row and was supposed to be executed at 8 pm. However, there were rumors that he could be pardoned. The warden was summoned to the governor's office. The warden told the executioner that he would send him a message to inform him of the decision.

When the warden met the governor, he was told that new evidence had surfaced which suggested that the prisoner was innocent. The warden hastily sent a message to the executioner. It read, "Hang him, not wait for me." However, what he actually meant to type was, "Hang him not, wait for me."

He had misplaced the comma in his message and failed to check that detail. I do not need to tell you what happened next; this is why it is important to have a good eye for detail. These experiences are relatable in our daily lives. While writing a check, you could lose a lot of money if you do not verify the details; you might have added an extra zero by mistake. It is important to cultivate this trait and if you are in a leadership role, ensure that this becomes part of your team's work culture.

I remember coming across an incident involving Steve Jobs. One Sunday, Steve Jobs frantically called the Vice-President of Google. Jobs had noticed that there was a small error which no one in Google or Apple had identified. Jobs said, "I was looking at the Google logo on the iPhone, and I am not happy with the icon. The second O in Google doesn't have the right yellow gradient. It's just wrong, and I'm going to have it fixed right away. Is that okay with you?"

This was the obsessive care that Steve Jobs paid to his products. It is why he was one of the greatest entrepreneurs of the 20th century. He had a strong eye for detail, and he cared about every small detail. He was concerned with how one issue could provide the wrong impression.

This attention was distilled through the company that saw them develop revolutionary gadgets with Apple and spectacular animation films from Pixar.

He led from the front when it came to having a strong eye for detail. You should remember that having an eye for detail can make or break you. The lack of it can cause you to remain stagnant or be unsatisfied. It is a trait that is not explicitly mentioned as required in any job advertisement. However, as I learned from my CEO, you live it and embody it.

**Habits to Improve Your Eye for Detail**

There is some wisdom in the saying that you learn from your mistakes. I agree; mistakes should not create shame within you. It is just an indicator to show where you can improve. However, none of us wants to make mistakes, be it related to a job or a human connection. This is especially true in the professional sphere, where errors can be expensive for the individual and the organization. Hence, you must cultivate and improve your eye for detail.

As you improve, you will be able to find and catch issues before they become mistakes. You can avoid costly blunders in the short term and long term because you have your eyes peeled for every detail. This skill is paramount for any job or role you assume. Your job title does not matter; your skill should speak for you regardless.

Having been impressed by the importance of this skill, some of you may now wonder how to identify if you have it. I can tell you that there is no universally accepted method to determine if you have this skill. There are some ways you can decide if you have it.

I would recommend that you first check your resume. You would have sent it to your current employer, or you may send it to a future employer. There is a saying that first impressions are important.

Your resume is the first impression you make on a prospective employer. So, check your resume. Are there any spelling mistakes? Are there any typos that you did not notice? Is the formatting skewed in any of the lines? Are the fonts and font sizes consistent? Have you typed your resume in a weird font like comic sans? If you find that there are issues, you know that you need to work on your eye for detail.

Another method you could follow is to recall your last meeting or interview. You could have been the interviewer or the interviewee.

Try to remember the meeting. Were there times when your attention drifted? While speaking, did you branch out on tangents? Can you recall every minute? Were you distracted by some noises or sights outside your meeting zone?

If your answer was yes to any of these questions, you need to work on your eye for detail. These are mostly home-based tools to check your eye for detail. There are tools available in the market today that use cognitive assessment to measure your eye for detail. Many organizations use these tools today.

Organizations know that having an eye for detail is an invaluable asset for employees. They need proactive employees who can spot the error before it is committed. This trait can determine a company's profit or loss. If you are a leader, you can mentor your team members to use it in their daily lives. When you foster such a work culture, you are bound to march to success.

Therefore, if you are in a position to hire someone, place great emphasis on this trait. It is a vital skill that will only make you and your team and thus your company more robust and successful.

I have given many presentations in my life. However, there is one presentation that remains vivid in my memory. I had given this particular presentation in IIT, Delhi.

It is not memorable because of the content or the location. It became notable due to the feedback that I received. I was told that my presentation covered every base and left no scope for guesswork or imagination. I have been applauded for the meticulousness and comprehensive nature of my presentation.

I was elated. I had prepared it with great care and eye for detail. It was made with the experience I had accumulated over the years. It was ready for every possible question and area. I was happy that my attention to detail had paid off and that it was appreciated. It happens to be one of the best compliments that I have received.

Many experts and research studies show that organizations fail because they ignore the details. Problems arise because of this neglect. You can count the days if such neglect is the practice at senior levels of a company. If this scenario is to be avoided, I believe that paying attention to details and developing an 'Eye for detail' must be put into practice right from hiring. It should become standard practice and always be reviewed.

## How Can I Develop an Eye for Details?

I should warn you once again that this is not simply wished into existence. It is a skill, like any other, that needs to be developed and practiced daily.

It requires a tremendous amount of commitment, focus, and constant practice.

Here are simple ways to develop an eye for detail:

1. **The homework research:** You must approach every task with some foreknowledge. If you go in blind, you will only stumble around due to the lack of preparation. So, before you start any assignment, spend some time on homework. Research your work and do some background checks. If you are meeting a client, find out all the relevant information about them. What is their role, their education, or their preferred language for conversation? Should you be aware of any cultural markers?

There is a famous marketing fable about Coco-Cola. The story goes that a Coco-Cola marketing executive tried to market the renowned soft drink in the Middle East. Since he did not know the local language, he decided to use a creative tool. He had three images. The first image showed a man dying in the desert; the second image showed the dying man finding a bottle of Coco-Cola and drinking it.
The third image showed him re-energized. It was a brilliant visual form of storytelling. However, when he unveiled that particular slide, he was stunned to see the people in shock. He would only realize later that he had arranged these images to go left to the right.
However, reading in the Middle East is done from right to left. So, for the potential clients, the story was that a man full of energy drank a bottle of Coco-Cola and consequently was dying in the desert!
It is a comedic story but one can learn from that example. If you are presenting at a forum, find out your audience. Do a little research. Can you be esoteric? Should you perhaps make your content a bit simpler? You should pay attention; likewise, if you are speaking on any matter, do your research. Do not rely on any surface knowledge or hearsay.

2. **Use checklists:** Make a checklist after you do your preliminary research on any new project or venture. Note down what are the things that you need to know. What are the finer points that you find essential to be answered? When you make this checklist, you will miss nothing. Let us say, for instance, you have to interview a candidate for a job opening. In your checklist, you will have to include the candidate's CV. Does the candidate's profile match the job description? Where has the candidate worked previously? Do you have any information on these previous organizations? Are there any specific skills that you need to test? For example, if the role is in customer interface, how are the conflict management skills of the candidate? So, detail your interview. Be as exhaustive as you can while being relevant to the job profile. You can prepare for any task in advance. Incorporate the habit of creating a checklist so that you are ready for the task before you start.

3. **Recheck your work:** Always recheck and review your progress on any task. Do this step at least twice on any job. I follow a five-step review process. When you review, you may find details that you missed or points where you drifted away from the progress. For example, let us say you have to give a presentation. Have it ready well before time.

   Please have at least two rehearsals of the production before you present it in its final form. This review process will help you with the development of your eye for detail. You may find areas where your audience may have questions, and you must be prepared for them.

   You may also find questions for yourself that may need to be answered to make the presentation better.

4. **Chill out, take a break:** This is not a joke. It would be best if you took time to rest and refocus. If your mind is tired, you will miss details. If you do not take the time to relax your mind, you will be prone to miss details. Your mind will be exhausted, and you will not be able to concentrate. No one is immune from this condition.

   It would help if you recognized when your mind feels saturated. When you feel drained mentally, do something else. Take a walk, have a cup of coffee, or read your favorite book for a while. Do some activity that will energize you. When you come back refreshed, you will be refocused with a keener eye for detail.

5. **Do not rush:** On a related thought, do not rush when you are doing your tasks. It is a sign of impatience and will cause you to miss important details. Some of you may struggle with time management when it comes to reviews and progressing on your task.

   Therefore, you must plan your lessons accordingly. Rank the tasks based on priority, and when you schedule accordingly, you will find that you will have enough time to realize your deliverables with reviews.

As I have mentioned, developing your eye for detail is not something that you wish into existence. It cannot be built over in one or two days. It is a daily exercise that needs constant minding.

Think of it as a muscle exercise. It would help if you worked on it regularly. So, follow the tips I have mentioned in this chapter, and you will soon see the quality of your work greatly improve. You will stand out from the rest due to the excellent nature of your work.

If you are a job seeker, know these aspects will be evaluated as part of your eye for detail:

- The job application and resume itself.
- Well-structured, error-free resume, with consistent formatting.
- Ability to quickly detect an error or mistake in language, tenses, grammar, etc.
- Error-free content writing, blog writing, and article writing, etc.
- Skill to review different types of documents for accuracy.
- Skill to observe and share findings (if asked) about the office's ambience or the organization.
- Key findings on the organization's website.

Let us look at the following instances from day-to-day life.

- The pilot is in charge of hundreds of people who have shown confidence in his ability to take them to their destination safely. If the pilot has a keen eye for detail, they could be like Captain Chesley Sullenberger, who landed the plane safely on the Hudson River when he lost both the engines on his plane following a bird hit. If they do not have the same eye for detail, they could crash the plane.

- A share broker or trader has to have an eye for detail to keep checking the negative and positive trends in the market and ensure their investors do not go bankrupt.

- An accountant has to have an eye for detail to ensure they make error-free calculations. Their calculations will ensure that organizations do not suffer from any losses in any manner, owing to wrong measures.

- A banker is entrusted with thousands of people's life savings. They are supposed to practice an eye for detail before launching any scheme or interest rate projections so that neither the customer nor their bank suffers. You need to look no further than some of the bad loans given out by bankers to some industrialists.

- A surgeon is completely trusted to work with an extreme eye for detail when operating on a patient lying unconscious under anesthesia. They cannot afford to lose their eye for detail at any point during the surgery as it could prove fatal.

These are just a few examples from our day-to-day life. The fact is, any leader in a leadership role must possess and exhibit an eye for detail, owing to the responsibility they have, and in turn, continue creating stories of success.

For working on yourself to develop an eye for detail, let us use the following table to work out:

| Find Your Godfather Inside You | Eye for detail | Write Here |
|---|---|---|
| Learning Exercise | Write down a task or a project that you are currently working at, or are about to start working at, or want to work at. | Create a checklist on what all do you want to have incorporated into it, including your homework research:<br>1.<br>2.<br>3.<br>4.<br>5.<br>6.<br>7.<br>8.<br>9.<br>10. |
| | Check on the decided checklist as you progress in your task, every day, in the following manner | |
| | Follow-up check for practice thrice daily for 10 days | |

|  |  |  |
|---|---|---|
|  | – morning, afternoon, night |  |
|  | Follow-up check for practice twice daily for 10 days – morning, night |  |
|  | Follow-up check for practice once daily once for 10 days, at night |  |

*You can devise as many tables like above as possible, task wise, and check your progress. This practice will help you develop a strong eye for detail.

I learned the importance of having an eye for detail on that fateful day when I went with my CEO on the facility inspection round. You may not have realized the great importance of this trait yet, but I hope this chapter helps you build a robust and careful eye for detail. When you have an eye for detail, it is your basics that get strengthened. You may have seen buildings collapse in the news these days. They collapsed because they did not have strong foundations. So, when you have an eye for detail, you have a strong base, and you will be able to stand firm in the face of storms and adverse weather conditions. I am sure your inner Godfather has always been hinting at you to work on this skill. However, you may tend to ignore this request. I hope this chapter helps you listen to your inner voice and implement this practice. Do this, and you will be able to convert yourself into a strong professional, a good human being, and a successful leader.

# 10
## STRONG FOUNDATION
### Forging roots to weather winds of change

*"Everyone loves to create ideas but fewer build upon solid foundations of thought."* — C.A.A. Savastano

### The Importance of Firm Foundations

When I say the word 'foundation', what pops into your mind? The first image that will probably come to your mind will be that of dug-up earth. When a new structure or building is being constructed, the builders dig deep into the earth to lay the foundation. They do so to provide stability to the structure or building. It is the first step in the construction process and incidentally also the most crucial one. The sustainability and durability of the structure depend on how secure its foundations are. If there is a misstep in laying the foundation, the very resilience and reliability of the structure will be compromised. So, it is essential to have a good strong foundation. It is the foundation that enables a building to stand tall in the face of heavy rains or other extreme natural conditions.

When you see news reports of a building collapse following heavy rains or floods, you will hear reports of shoddy construction. However, the truth is that the particular building's foundation was probably compromised; the root of the issue would be shoddy work from the foundation itself. If the foundation is flawed, no amount of glam-up on the edifice of a structure will suffice.

The structure is flawed fundamentally and it is sure to come crashing down on one momentous day. The strong foundation of any building determines the structure's future; similarly, success, especially sustainable success, of any leader depends on a deep, strong foundation, just like that of a building. Let us suppose the foundation is weak and not deep enough. In that case, the building will not sustain longer, and will eventually succumb to any of nature's fury and havoc. A leader (or even an organization) who might have attained success for any reason will perish fast if the foundation is not deep and strong enough.

If we are talking about a person, his or her foundation is the sum of their values and personality. It is formed from the formative years as a toddler to the age of adulthood. The upbringing of a child can play a huge role in their development. How was the child brought up? What were the influencing factors during the child's growth? Were the parents strict or did they adopt a laissez-faire approach in their parenting? Who were the other influential people around the child? What kind of schooling did the child have? As mentioned in the previous chapters, my father's core values have become a part of my foundation. All these aspects work in the making of an individual's personality.

These factors play a role in the construction of your personal identity. However, what about your professional identity? Where and when is the foundation for this personality laid? The immediate, obvious answer could be when you start your first job. However, it starts much earlier. It starts in your teenage years. The background for your personal identity starts from your childhood as you learn to imitate the world and find your place. Similarly, you get the first inkling of responsibility and its associated ideas when you are a teenager. You know that you are going to become an adult soon. Like the toddler looking to imitate the world, you too look to professionals for examples. However, it does not mean that you will not learn anything when you start your career. I want my teenage readers and others who have started their professional lives to particularly understand the importance of having a solid foundation. When you do not have a solid foundation, you will not live up to your full potential. I always knew that I needed to have my basics right. Perhaps it is another legacy from the professional side of my father. A judge cannot pass a judgment until all the facts are presented.

I always worked to have the basics straightened out. I knew that to progress further professionally, I had to reinforce my basics. It was especially important when I assumed leadership roles. Even when I mentor some of my colleagues, it is the one thing that I stress on.

They have to work on strengthening their foundations.

For instance, I used to interview junior doctors as part of my role in Medical Administration. I enjoyed asking them basic questions rather than asking tricky and confusing questions that would tie them in knots. I would always ask them basic questions at first. It would give me an idea of their capabilities as a doctor.

So, I would ask questions like, "How do you take the pulse readings?", "Why do you use three fingers for pulse measurement?", "What's the normal blood pressure level?", etc. Many would answer the last question as 120/80 mmHg. This answer would be fine for your average person. However, it is an unacceptable answer for a doctor. You would not believe me, but many doctors fail in answering these basic questions correctly. You might also be curious why I stress on strengthening the basics and ask junior doctors such questions?

I use this approach to gauge not just the knowledge deficit in the candidate. I can also evaluate the attitude of the person based on these questions. There should be a hunger in them to consolidate the basics. Such an attitude cannot be taught. It comes from an inner hunger to fill in the gaps. Look at any successful comeback in sports. It could be even cricket. When an out-of-form batsman suddenly scores a century, he will always be asked about how he returned to form. Invariably, the answer will involve a variation of the idea that he returned to his basics.

This hunger to return to the basics and consolidate them is driven by the desire to not get stuck when faced with challenging situations. They know at the root of any superlative and sustainable success lies a strong foundation built on having the basics right. This is a trait that is shared by every successful leader. Leaders do not become successful only by leading their teams during times of comfort. They become successful because they are able to lead during tough scenarios. They are prepared to endure adversities and lead the team under dire circumstances. They can do so because they are firm in their basics. They may not know every function to the last detail, but they will know enough to discuss with the relevant team member and draft an action plan.

For instance, a marketing manager must have the basic knowledge of costing to understand budgeting and the expenses involved in a marketing campaign. Leaders who do not have a strong foundation are found out quickly and fail. So, if you want to be a successful leader, consolidate your basics and build a strong foundation.

Once you have identified your goal, it is important that you build a solid foundation geared for the particular goal. Let us suppose that you want to become a film director. You should know the basics of camera work, sound design, editing, production, etc. You need to know the basics of all aspects of filmmaking. You may pose the argument that it is not necessary to know the basics of all these aspects. However, a film is the product of the vision of a director. Can you entrust others to realize your vision? While there may be specialists, you need the basic knowledge to translate your vision across to them. You need to know the basics to ensure that you are on a steady rise to the top instead of peaking one moment and then crashing down to smithereens. A deep, robust foundation will prop you up when you face challenges and leave you standing even after your circumstances threaten to slam you down. A good foundation will also keep you grounded because when your mind is focused on the basics, it will not let you be intoxicated by the heights of success.

Let me reinforce the importance of a good foundation:

- Working toward laying a strong foundation is the basic step for long-term success, and it encompasses every single trait (described in previous chapters) that is required to be a successful leader
- Having a strong foundation is an attitude—a positive attitude

Your foundation is not just a marker of your professional competency; it is also a marker of your personal maturity. Your personal traits get reflected in your work. It shows how you treat other people and interact with them. It also indicates how you handle pressure and critical situations. One of the best examples I can suggest is from the sport of cricket. Think of batsmen like MS Dhoni, Michael Bevan, or Michael Hussey. They were known as finishers amidst all the pomp and show of one-day cricket.

However, you could see how they handled the pressure.
They stuck to the basics with singles and doubles to keep the scoreboard ticking with an occasional big shot. They only unleashed the fury in the final overs when needed.

While they were fierce competitors, you could see their characters reflected in their playing. They were calm and unruffled. Their calmness would reflect in their game. It is this calmness that allowed them to succeed where many others would have failed. Your foundation is the reflection of your personality.

A strong foundation is based on these core values:

## Core values

- Passion
- Honesty
- Understanding responsibility and accountability (being reliable, dependable)
- Self confidence
- Your values
- Integrity
- Determination
- Being empathetic and compassionate
- Commitment
- Being caring
- Principles
- Discipline
- Sincerity
- An eye for detail
- Knowledge and willingness to learn
- Your overall character
- Focus

All these traits are necessary to build a strong foundation for any type of success in your life. You cannot compromise on any of these traits. You need to focus on all of them and use them to build yourself.

When you have a foundation built on these qualities, you will be ready to face any kind of problem in your life. You could be swaying like grass in the face of strong winds of fate and change. However, when these traits are inculcated in you, you will stay rooted and ride out the turbulence; these qualities will enable you to always stay stable and succeed in life.

It is a fast-changing world that we live in and with the digital age, change is always just around the corner.

A strong foundation based on these core values will ensure that you are unshakeable. A strong foundation provides structure in your life. It will keep you from being overwhelmed.

These traits and values, reinforced by your habits, will help you develop a strong mindset A strong foundation will enhance your strengths and help transform your weaknesses into opportunities. You will also feel more secure in your relationships when you have a foundation based on these traits.

> *"Building your foundation isn't a one-time event. Habits will slip and you will need to rebuild them periodically. Your goals may change, forcing you to change your foundation to suit them. But if you've spent the time investing in a foundation initially, these changes are maintenance, not a complete reconstruction."* – Scott H. Young

## One-hit Wonders vs. Sustainable Successes

There are many instances of one-time success stories or one-hit wonders. There is the example of Vinod Kambli. He was a flamboyant batsman compared to the classical stylist in Sachin Tendulkar. However, Sachin had a more robust foundation built on all the traits I have mentioned. Kambli made a big splash initially, but was soon consigned to the pages of history as just another has-been. He is not alone. There have been many cricketers who announced their presence with a bang but failed to establish themselves in the national side. There are other examples from the film industry. There are many actors who made a big splash when one of their movies turned into a huge hit.

We would have expected them to reach great heights, but they never were as successful again. Their movies never became hits on the same scale again. Some of their films may have become slightly popular, but they would never scale the same heights again. Why?

If you look at their films critically, you will find that their debut film would have become a major success due to other factors like an excellent script or even an extremely memorable soundtrack. It may also be that their deficiencies were well-camouflaged in that film. However, once they stepped out of that film, their shallow foundations were exposed. They may have possessed the movie star looks, but their lack of basics would see them fall short. Probably their acting skills were not good enough or they were not good at emoting and displayed wooden expressions. Whatever the reason, they were unable to portray the depth of character required for various roles. The reasons for failure may be many, but underlying them all is the shallow foundation in their chosen field.

On the flip side, there are many actors who do not possess classic movie star looks. However, they are extremely popular and marketable. Their name would suffice to sell out movie theatres. If you trace their journey, you will find that their foundations are solid. They may have spent time playing various roles in local theatres and would have acted in dramas on the stage. They would have committed time to hone their acting skills, and this preparation translates across to the cameras.

They are successful in making a mark for themselves. They are known for their talent and for being selective in choosing good-quality film scripts that challenge them. They practice excellence and push themselves. There is no ego in them. They keep looking for roles that would be challenging to them as actors. They keep improving their craft. When Mahesh Narayanan and Fahadh Faasil were quizzed about the high quality of Malayalam films, they replied that the foundation of Malayalam movies was good literature. Unlike many movies in Hollywood and Bollywood, Malayalam films are not driven by star presence and charisma.

These are examples of how you can be led astray. History is rife with examples of one-hit wonders. They are now dismissed as flukes. Their success will be remembered as the result of a gimmick rather than the person's achievement. Do you want to join that list? If you do not wish to join their company, it is vital that you look to build and reinforce your foundation.

## Dictations and Dispositions

I recall an incident from my childhood about my father who was always a picture of serenity and patience. However, on one extremely rare occasion, I saw my father lose his temper.

He was trying to dictate something to Mr. Kowli, his personal assistant, who was also his stenographer. I think Mr. Kowli had committed a mistake. I do not remember the exact reason. But I heard my father speak in a very stern voice.

He did not need to raise his voice or scream at the top of his lungs. The man known for his patience was stern in his feedback. It was a clear indication that he was upset. This happened in the office which was situated in the house. Then I saw my father ask Mr. Kowli to go out and take a walk. He asked him to take his time and have a glass of tea or a glass of water and then return to resume work.

I witnessed the incident and was determined to stay away for the time being. The next morning, I accompanied my father on his morning walk. I am being generous when I say I accompanied my father. As mentioned in one of the previous chapters, I was not really a morning person. However, my father was trying to instill the habit into me. So, he used to wake me up and ask me to accompany him. On that morning, he spoke of the incident with Mr. Kowli. I could see that he was troubled about having displayed his anger. He was upset that he had behaved in such a manner and it was still affecting him the next morning. I could not understand why he was upset. From my viewpoint, Mr. Kowli did commit a mistake and my father had the right to be angry with him.

Then my father said a few words that made a deep impression on me. This thought is now part of my core and a vital aspect of my foundation. He said, "Son, one must be good to everyone, irrespective of their status. Try to make the time they spend with you good so that they look forward to being with you. There could be occasions where you have to be critical when people commit a mistake. However, when you treat everyone well, there is very little scope for such mistakes being committed. If such a mistake is indeed committed, do not roll over and compromise. Call them out and point out their mistakes so that they do not repeat them. Their carelessness can sometimes affect someone else far more severely. So, it is important that we be serious and sober when the situation demands.

However, when you are being critical of them, they should not feel as if they are being trampled on. You are criticizing just that one deed or action. Never make them feel that they are flawed completely. Never make them feel that they are incompetent or bad." I was surprised. But how could one be assured that pointing out blame was not a reflection on the personality or the person?

My father sensed my dilemma. He continued, "Once you have pointed out their error, make sure that you become normal and affectionate with them. Then they will know that the criticism was for the action and not the individual. When you return to behaving normally, they will know that the moment is over and that you trust them to not repeat it. Nobody is bad all the time. You just have to mix and match according to the circumstances."

My father then explained the situation with Mr. Kowli. He did not explain the details of the issue as his profession involved confidentiality. He had to keep such matters confidential. He just indicated to me that Mr. Kowli had gotten a couple of things wrong in his assignment as he had not understood the concept. Some lives were at stake on that assignment and that is why my father was upset with that action of Mr. Kowli's.

Unknowingly, I had adopted the same practice in my professional career as well. Many years after that incident, I was stepping out of a business review conference in the boardroom. One of my colleagues approached me. I smiled and he seemed a bit taken aback. He then explained to me that when I was in the boardroom, I was a different person. Whenever I participated in any business review work, I would become a different personality.

I could not understand what he was driving at. He then explained to me that outside the review meetings, I was often jovial and lighthearted. I seemed a world apart from the severe authority figure who went through the review meetings. He even elaborated that I was an extremely gregarious and welcoming person 95 percent of the time. I would often crack jokes and even pull the occasional prank. I was self-deprecating sometimes and I would laugh a lot with my colleagues. This was the case even when I trained or mentored them. However, he said that the remaining five percent of the time I was very sober and strict. The laugh lines in my face would have disappeared. This time was when I reviewed the operations with a great eye for detail. His narration amused me. He even provided me a breakdown in percentages!

However, later in the day, I remembered that morning walk with my father. I realized that I had based my behavior on those wise words bestowed on me by my father. It has been a regular part of my conduct in all professional and personal settings. Can you imagine the extremes of this behavior? What if you were strict all the time? Would you inspire any form of great teamwork?

Would it not make people more afraid of you and not approach you with any problems? There could be a distinct lack of human warmth in such a work culture. What if you were more lenient and indifferent to mistakes? Would the quality of your team's work be good? Would you be sending a signal that they could compromise on their work as you would not call them out on it?

Both these scenarios are not ideal, and in some cases, could also be disastrous. It is up to you to find that balance. There is no ideal mix. As my colleague had noted, I was strict five percent of the time. But I was strict at the key places and more fun and open the rest of the time. My father may not have borne witness to my career. However, his teachings have accompanied me and have become a crucial part of my foundation. My inner Godfather has been inspired by the learnings that were imparted to me by my father.

## Deep Foundations are Seldom Damaged

There is this old tale that is still popular that lets us know that a strong foundation will never be devalued. There was a renowned speaker who used to give seminars to motivate and mentor people. One day, he was speaking to an audience of about 100 people. He started the seminar by holding up a check for Rs 10,000. He said that the check was made out to the bearer of it. Even as people were wondering, he raised a question. "Who among you would like to be the bearer of this check and encash the amount?"

All 100 members of the audience raised their hands. Who would not like to get money unasked? However, the speaker just smiled. He then said, "Keep your hands raised if you still would like to have the check, no matter what I do." He then crumpled it in front of the audience. He then asked the crowd, "So, do you still want it?" All the 100 hands remained in the air. He then dropped it on the ground and stomped on it. He was dirtying the check. He then picked it up and unrolled it to show it to the audience. The camera also zoomed in on the note to display it on the big screen.

The audience could see that the check was still intact materially. Although it was no longer in pristine condition as there were creases and dirt smudged across it, the details entered were still legible. The speaker then asked again, "How many of you still want it?" The hands remained in the air despite a few giggles. The speaker smiled and said, "My dear friends, I have shown you one of the fundamental lessons in life. When I showed you a brand-new check, all of you wanted it.

It is understandable. However, when I crumpled it, you still wanted it. I tested you further when I dirtied it using the sole of my shoe. You still wanted it. It was crumpled and dirty and yet you shared the same enthusiasm to want it. Your enthusiasm and desire did not abate one iota. Why is that? You could see that despite its bad condition, it was still legal tender. The value of that check had not reduced despite the material changes to it.

You could have encashed the 10,000 rupees regardless. Similarly, in life, there will be occasions when you will be crumpled. There will be occasions when you go through the wringer and come out dusty and dirty. You should aim to be like the check whose value was not devalued by the external circumstances. Never allow your circumstances to devalue or demean you.

You can only attain that status when you have a strong foundation. If you have a weak foundation, you will be left tattered by the wayside. It is vital, ladies and gentlemen, that you do not lose your worth. Stay calm and positive and rely on your robust foundation during challenging times, and when you come through, you will find that your foundation has ensured that your values remained unscathed."

Be like the check that could still hold its value despite the state it was in. Your foundation is what determines your worth and potential. While there can be occasions when you have to make changes, your foundation should remain solid. Your core values must be valued and remain uncompromised. You can reinforce them with additional qualities. The importance of your values cannot be discounted. I remember another story that I had read.

James was an aspirational student. He came from a well-off family. However, he was diligent in his studies and wanted to do his best. When he was in college, he visited a car showroom. The latest sports car was on display. He was quite taken up by it. He spent an inordinate amount of time just gawking at it.

He knew he wanted to have that car. So, when he went home that evening, he told his parents that he wanted that car as his graduation gift. He made this statement because he knew that his parents could easily afford that car. He studied hard to ensure that he passed with flying colors.

It did not come as a surprise when he did accomplish the same. Soon it was his graduation day. He donned the graduation robe with great relish. He was more excited about getting his new car than attending the actual function. He had built up a lot of anticipation.

He had also bragged to a few friends that he would be receiving the car as a graduation gift. He waited for the official photography session to end, and then went home expecting to find the keys to the new car. However, when he returned home, he could see no sign of the car. His father then presented a rectangular box. His father said, "I am very proud of you, Son." However, James barely heard him.

He saw that the package was exquisitely gift-wrapped. He could see that the box was slightly big to hold a box of car keys. He was disappointed. However, he still opened the package with apprehension. There was also a slight inkling of desperate hope that he would find the car keys inside as part of an elaborate prank. He ripped open the package as if ripping away a band-aid.

He found himself holding a leather-bound Bible. He could not believe his eyes. He placed the Bible on the table and exploded in rage. He shouted, "You are so rich. You could easily afford that car. I have never demanded anything extravagant in my life previously. I studied so hard to ensure that I would be able to drive that car. Now, you give me a Bible! How could you?"

Tears streamed down his face as he could not control his rage and sadness. He walked out of his house. He became estranged from his father on that day. He soon found a job and new accommodations. He never spoke to his father ever again.

Even the passage of time did not decrease the resentment he felt toward his father. He did invite his father to his wedding, but he never spoke to him. James had become a successful businessman and even had two beautiful children from a very happy marriage. His fatherhood only made him resent his father who would not give his son a sports car as a graduation gift. He thought that he would do anything for his children, but his father did not do the same. Then on one fateful day, he received a telegram. His father had passed away and the will was in his father's house.

James carried out the last rites of his father. He only returned to his father's house after his father was buried in the cemetery. He looked at the house and soon went from one room to another. He then entered his father's study hoping to find the will. However, he found his graduation gift. The Bible was on the table. Some of the gift wrapper that was not ripped out was still attached to the gift. The colors had faded. However, he could see that it was still untouched. His eyes brimmed with tears without his knowledge. He was engulfed with sadness for not having communicated with his father for so many years.

He opened the Bible and found a verse that was underlined by his father. It read, "*And if ye, being evil, know how to give good gifts to your children, how much more shall your Heavenly Father give to those who ask Him?*" Even as he tried to comprehend the meaning of the verse, an object fell with a thud from the book. He bent down and found himself grasping a car key.

While his mind scrambled to make the connection, he found a note attached to it. It was a faded paper that had withstood the ravages of time. The note had a date. It was the date of his graduation. There were a few words written as well. He struggled to read them through his tears. It read, "Paid in full, for my loving son."

The story impresses on how we should value what we have. Believe in your parents and trust them. James turned away from his father due to a sports car. In the end, he realized his mistake. He found the car. However, it was heavily weighed down with guilt and regret as he could never recover the lost years with his father due to his petulance.

Your foundation is the source of your unshakeable spirit. It will be the beacon of light that will dispel the darkness in your life. When you are presented with choices in your life, your foundation will help you choose the option that would work the best for you. It is the basis of your character.

Your character is important as it will help determine how you live your life. When you have a weak foundation, you are likely to make choices that are weak. It will only lead you to indulge in negative thoughts and encourage emotions of self-loathing and self-pity. You may find yourself mired in the swamp of victim mentality. Even when you manage to muster a little bit of confidence, your doubts will wash it away. You will be stuck in a regressive loop of negative emotions and actions.

So, how can you determine the basis of your foundation? It involves all the traits that I mentioned earlier. However, they can be summed up under these major categories:

- **Values:** Consider what values are important to you. Which of your values will you never compromise on?
- **Mindfulness:** Consider the quality of your thoughts.
- **Habits:** Consider your daily routine and patterns.
- **Strengths**: What are your strongest aspects? What are you good at?
- **Relationships**: Consider your relationships at all levels, be it personal or professional. In whose company do you feel good? In which relationships do you feel supported?

Now that I have given you these five categories, I want you to write down the answers to the questions that I have raised.

Once you have written the answers, I want you to consider one more thing. Which of the items that you have written is subject to change? Are there any items that you would reconsider? For instance, if you have been brought up as a pure vegetarian, you would probably consider your vegetarianism to be a value. But will you be tempted to try non-vegetarian fare? Is your resolve to maintain your vegetarian diet just as strong? On a related thought, you could be a teetotaler.

But will you have a drink or two, due to peer pressure? You could also say you are in a good relationship with your partner. Will you feel the same a year from now? You might have said you are good at painting. Are you in your best form as a painter? Do you think you can enhance your skills even more?

These are examples of how things and events in your life can change your perspectives in life. Are you stable in your beliefs and values? If you find yourself wavering, there is something wrong with your convictions. It means that there is a flaw in your foundation. There is a weakness that makes you doubt yourself.

Let us examine these categories in some more detail. What are values? Values, put simply, are your personal convictions that make you think and act in a certain way. There is a moral implication to your values. I have listed some of the values to make it clearer:

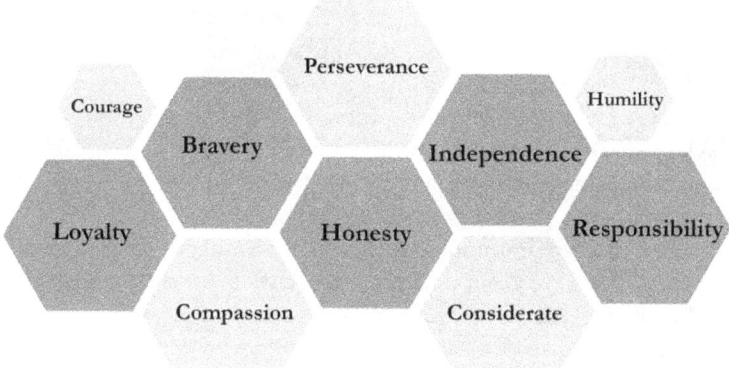

These values must be firm in your life.

If you find that your behavior on the above qualities changes depending on the situation or person, you do not have a stable foundation. Do not be a chameleon. You are bound to lose yourself once you keep donning different masks. People with firm foundations behave the same with everyone. They do not measure the value of a situation or person and the benefit that can be reaped from them. They are more concerned about remaining true to their values.

My son once taught me the lesson of perseverance. He was trying to record a song. He got the opportunity to record it in a professional recording studio. I knew he would do well as he had always been diligent and hardworking. He could have tripped up on the pride that he got the chance to record in a reputed studio. I used to accompany him to the studio every evening after my work shift ended.

This meant that we generally went to the studio late in the evenings and on Sundays. This event took place during the summer. The weather was hot, but this did not deter him. However, I would only recognize the perseverance of my son after a few days. He had not yet finished recording the song. I was wondering why it was taking so long. So, I stepped into the room with the recording booth. I was surprised to see him sweating and his shirt was drenched in sweat. He was talking with the audio engineer. The audio engineer was asking him to take a break. However, my son refused. He was adamant that he would not rest until he got his take right.

I found out later that my son was dissatisfied with his takes and want to get it right. He wanted to ensure that the meanings and the emotions behind the lyrics of the song were conveyed. He was insistent on getting it right. As my son sipped water from a bottle, I turned to the engineer and pointed to the air conditioner. It was switched off. He replied that ambient background sounds could affect the recording negatively. I sat and watched my son record multiple takes.

He was single-minded in his perseverance. He continued this despite many suggestions at various times from the engineer to take a break. He persisted and got it recorded as he wanted. It was a professional recording and I could not be prouder of him. However, he also showed me how one has to be single-minded in one's quest to produce quality work. He showed me his perseverance.

**What Constitutes Mindfulness?**

Ask yourself these questions and you will find the answer. It is the mental make-up of your life.

- Are you suspicious of people and situations? Do you have doubts regarding the intentions of people around you?
- Do you waste a lot of time thinking of regrets? Do you find it hard to move on from an unpleasant scenario or person?
- Do fantasies impact your decision-making process?
- Do you find it hard to understand your feelings and thoughts? Can you not trace the source of this discord within you?

Answer these questions honestly. If you find that your answer is yes to any of these questions, you need to work on your foundation.

Ask yourself the following questions on your habits. It is important that you understand the habits that make up your life.

Do not be blindly adherent to them. You need to question them to work on your foundation.

- What are your daily habits?
- Do you change your daily routine every few days/months? It could be as simple as your sleeping times.

- Are your habits good for your health? Do they reflect well on you, your family, and your profession?

If you find that you change your daily routine regularly, it indicates a lifestyle determined by impulses rather than will. You need to have stable habits to have a robust foundation.

Let us now examine your strengths.

- What are your biggest strengths?
- Do you think these strengths help or support you in your life?
- Do you think your strengths keep changing every few days? Are you plagued by bouts of doubt? Do you keep changing your idea of what your strengths are? Do you find the practice to enhance your strengths tiresome and move on to something else?

Some of you may think that you have no strengths worth speaking about. That is a problem. Similarly, if you constantly find working on your strengths tiresome, it is another problem. If you let your strengths stagnate without striving to enhance them, it is a waste. Such attitudes can be harmful to your foundation.

Ask yourself these questions to understand the depth and strength of your relationships.

- What do you think makes you feel comfortable in a relationship? (List them for all kinds of relationships such as friendships, familial relationships, love relationships, and professional relationships)
- What makes you feel happy in a relationship?
- Do you believe in moving on every few months or years? Do you think you become less interested in a relationship sooner when compared to others?

Are you unsure of the answers to the first two questions, and is your answer to the latter two is, yes? Then you need to work on your foundation.

Now that you know where you lack in these five categories, let us explore ways in which you can work on these deficiencies and reinforce your foundation.

I am sure you know of the famous tale of the three pigs and the wolf. One pig made its house of sticks and another pig made its house of straws.

Only the third pig took the time to dig and put in the foundations and then build a house made out of bricks. When the wolf came to their doors, he was able to blow down the first two houses and devour the two pigs. However, no matter how hard the wolf huffed and puffed, he could not shake the third house. Let us be like the third pig in the story. Let us take time to examine our foundations and reinforce them where they are weak. Your foundation is your invisible knight. It is the inner Godfather who guides you on your path. It warns you of things that may not be visible at first sight.

There are five important attributes that you need to develop to strengthen your foundation:

- Determination
- Resilience
- Habits
- Attitudes
- Focus

These five attributes drive your daily habits, behaviors, and decision-making processes. If you need to improve on these three factors in your life, it is essential that you work from the building blocks of those five attributes. When you pursue sustainable success, you need to answer the three 'Ws'. They will explain your motivations and help you break down your ambitions into achievable goals. Success cannot be just the fruit of hope and hard work. Even if you attain success in such cases, you will feel a lack of satisfaction. Hence, it is important to investigate your intentions and purposes.

1. **Why:** Ask yourself why? Why do you have a certain belief? What is the root cause for this belief? Subject every belief that you hold to a rigorous examination. Ask yourself why you believe in such an idea?

If it is a positive belief, reinforce the idea within yourself that you have to be consistent with it. If it is a negative belief, investigate the reasons behind it. Once you identify those reasons, work on them. Challenge the perceptions that inspire such a belief.

2. **Who:** Who are you? What constitutes you, my dear reader? Ask yourself a few questions to understand yourself. It is vital that you know more about yourself before you undertake any challenge.
   - What do you hold dear?
   - What are your beliefs?
   - What are your habits?
   - Who are the people that inspire you?
   - When you meet someone new or are in a new situation, what do you focus on at first? Do you look at the positives or negatives?

3. **What:** The legendary basketball coach John Wooden once commented, *"Be more concerned with your character than your reputation, because your character is what you really are, while your reputation is merely what others think you are."* These words are relevant as we are more concerned with our image than ourselves. You want to appear in a certain way and that negatively impacts you. When you are more worried about what others think of you, you relegate yourself to the back. Consequently, you send a signal to yourself that you are not that important. To maintain this guise that you wish to wear, you compromise on yourself and stop being honest with yourself. Pay greater attention to yourself and your character. Be more concerned with who you are and not who you want to be. The successful leaders in the world today blazed a path because they did not concern themselves with what others thought of them. When you concentrate on yourself, you will find that the traits of honesty and integrity are like second nature to you.

I understand that when you are looking to cause a fundamental change, you will have trouble beginning.

You may second-guess yourself. You may be worried about challenging your status quo. Bravely march forward. You may also encounter the challenge of holding on to the change in the long run. Changes of this nature are never quick and there can be no immediate self-gratification. You may struggle with motivation. Here is an example of how a lack of motivation will keep you from your goal.

Let us assume that you are trying to lose weight and become physically fit. You may be enthused in the beginning. You may enroll yourself in the best gymnasiums and consult the best nutritionists for diet guidance. You may find the energy to go to the gym regularly for a few days or weeks. You may also be further encouraged when you see a drastic loss of weight in the beginning within a short span of time. However, after a few days, you will find that you are not losing weight at the same rate. This may worry you for a while and you may lose your motivation. Another challenge could be procrastination when you work on a task.

You need to remember that a strong foundation will always be your savior during challenging times and guarantee you excellent long-term results. As explained in the example above, it can be challenging as there are no immediate visible results when you are working on your foundations. It is vital that we work on our foundations in a structured way. I have to add that it is important to have the patience to go along with your determination. Be relaxed about it and do not expect to see a change within you immediately. When you are working on your foundations, you are challenging your core beliefs and working to remodel your habits.

The results of your efforts will take time to develop. If I were to extend the example of the third pig from the story of the three pigs, you are 're-laying' every single brick in your house. Be patient, a few bricks do not make a house.

It may even take years to realize the changes within you. So, discard the expectations of change. Instead, focus on the process of working on every brick so that you can build a sturdy life for yourself.

There are three elements that need your attention when you are looking to reinforce and improve your foundation:

1. Becoming Organized
2. Your Daily Routine

3. Your Physical Fitness

**Becoming Organized:** Some of you may scoff at this idea. You could say that you are an organized person. Some of you may be organized in some situations and not so organized in others. The cheekier among you would even claim that what others see as chaos, is organized as per your view.

There is one way to test this idea. Look at your desk. How organized is it? Are there materials that need not be there? Is there any clutter? Where are the files, loose papers, pens, books, etc.? Look at your computer. Are there files in there that are not needed anymore? How cluttered is your desktop? Where do you save files? Do you backup your important documents? When did you last open your downloads folder? Do you delete files that are not needed anymore? How about your bed? Did you make your bed after you woke up this morning? The answers to these questions will tell you how organized you are. Remember that your physical surroundings are important. They play a significant role in influencing your mind.

When there is order around you, you generally reciprocate in kind. I must share that I am always very organized when it comes to my workplace. I learned it from the facility visit of the CEO. I was adamant that no clutter should be lying around in my office. I encouraged such behavior and attitude in my staff as well. However, when it came to my personal life, I was not that strict about it. I was a lot more relaxed when it came to my personal domain. However, I learned the importance of organization in my private life from my daughter.

She is the strongest person in terms of temperament in my family. One day, I asked myself how she was able to be so strong. Then I saw its visual representation in our house. She had a place for each of her belongings. The books would go to a certain place. The stationery and backup stationery had a place of their own.

She never compromised in sticking to this structure. There could be days when we come back exhausted and sleep in our work clothes. Sometimes we would shed them on the floor and plan to take care of them the next day. My daughter never compromised on these counts. She ensured that her life was organized and it is from that structure that she found her strength. That is how a non-cluttered environment can make a tremendous difference in your overall mindset.

**Your Daily Routine:** Make a note of your daily routine and check if this routine contributes to your goals. Find out what activities in your daily routine are not necessary. The aim is to streamline your routine and eliminate unnecessary practices. If you look at successful sports teams, they talk of the importance of repetitions in practice. Know that excellence comes from practice.

Let us assume that your struggle is with punctuality. You are generally late to the office in the mornings. You may trace the reason to the city traffic. However, dig deeper. Why is it that you get stuck in the traffic? Could you pack your breakfast and have it in your office? You would probably have to make an earlier start to beat the traffic. How about if you prepare your breakfast the previous night and heat it in the morning? Are there activities that delay your departure? Do you spend time reading the newspaper or indulge in some neighborly gossip? Can you eliminate these habits in the morning so that you can save time and instead do these when you are at leisure? So, check your routine and look at how you can refine them.

**Your Physical Fitness:** It is vital that you have a healthy and physically fit body. There is the adage that a sound mind resides in a sound body. You need to be physically fit to provide the energy required for your day. You need the strength and stamina to go about your day. When you are looking to effect a fundamental change, it is important to have an abundant source of energy. I understand that if you are not physically fit, this process can be even tougher as you will have lower reserves of energy.

Thus, it is important that you work on your physical fitness. I would like to also remind you that when you work on your physical fitness, discard the expectation of quick results. Work on it and you will slowly find your reserves expand. You may think that these three earmarked areas are very basic. However, this is where you lay the foundation.

You need these basic ingredients for building a robust structure. The sturdier your ingredients are, the better your structure will be. It is vital that you work on these areas. They are pretty basic and quite easy to work on. Once you decide that you want to effect a fundamental change in your life, then commit to making improvements in these three areas. You can have milestones within these three larger conceptual areas.

They may be as listed:
- Make a productive morning ritual within your daily routine to help you be more productive.
- Keep a daily journal where you can identify small tasks to be accomplished. Cross them once completed. Analyze your journal regularly to check if you are able to meet these tasks daily or weekly.
- Make a list of healthy foods to be added to your diet; similarly include the foods you have to avoid.
- Schedule time for daily exercise; it would be even better if it is done regularly at the same time. Hence, schedule it keeping the feasibility of that in mind.
- Note new ideas that could help in strengthening your foundations. Do not ignore them.
- Remove time-wasting habits.
- Make a commitment for a few hours of relaxation, including adequate sleep.
- Review your progress on all these areas either daily or weekly. The journal would be of great help.

You may now pose a relevant question. How do I ensure that I remain committed to this process? The aforementioned tips will help you address your fundamental weaknesses in a structured manner. However, maintaining this process will be harder than you think. These changes will need time to become part of your nature and personality. There will be temptations to stray or have a cheat day. It is critical that you turn a deaf ear to such voices. Remain committed, and as I said earlier, remove the burden of expectations. Cultivate patience so that you are not demotivated by the lack of quick results. This is a test of your determination. There could be occasions when certain habits may need to be amended due to special circumstances.

To ensure that these changes are transitioned flawlessly, you need a thorough review process. This review process should be part of your routine when you are establishing these habits. When you constantly review your routine, you will instill discipline that will help you deal with any transitions to and fro. Let us say, you have developed the habit of waking up at 6 am. You chose this time as it would provide you with enough time to complete your morning ablutions and chores.

You get enough time to exercise and get ready for work. Now, assume you get a better opportunity at another company. However, this workplace is farther away from your house. You would now need to wake up at 5 am to get there on time. Or maybe you have a new project at work where you need to work based on American timings. These are transitions that need your review process to be flawless. When you subject yourself to a rigorous review process, you are sending yourself a signal that you are determined to make changes for the better. It also reminds you of your basics. Thus, when you have to make a change in your routine, this determination will ensure that your transition is smoother.

When you follow these steps, you will find that your productivity would have increased, be it in your job, business, studies, or even relationships. These incremental changes would boost your confidence to confront bigger issues and challenges. It would mark the start of your evolution.

I would like to reiterate the story of the three little pigs. There can be no quick success. Do not even think on those lines, no matter how alluring the fantasy can be. When the wolves come to the door, people may panic and lose control. Be the third pig: build your house with a strong foundation. Take the time, but build a sturdy one which can keep the wolves at bay.

I must stress that the bottom line must never change. When you want to build and reinforce your foundation, learn to be patient. You are building a house that can stand the test of time. Do not take shortcuts and do not compromise on your building blocks. Stay strong and stay true to yourself.

When you can maintain such a mindset, you will find that success, especially sustainable success, was never so easy to attain.

| Find Your Godfather Inside You | Strong Foundation | Write Here |
|---|---|---|
| Learning Exercise | Identify the depth of your foundations under these headings:<br>**Your Values**<br>**Your Mindfulness**<br>**Your Habits**<br>**Your Strengths**<br>**Your Relationships**<br><br>*(Please check the columns under the same headings above, to understand better) | Wherever you find you have a weak foundation under any of these five, write down the sub-goals you have decided to work on in your day-to-day living:<br>1.<br>2.<br>3.<br>4.<br>5.<br>6. |
| | Identify sub-tasks under the headings of:<br>**Becoming Organized**<br>**Your Daily Routine**<br>**Your Physical Fitness**<br><br>*(Please check the columns under the same headings above, to understand better) | Enlist the sub-tasks required to be done for these headings as below:<br>**Becoming Organized**<br>1.<br>2.<br>3.<br>4.<br>5.<br>6. |

|  |  | **Your Daily Routine**<br>1.<br><br>2.<br><br>3.<br><br>4.<br><br>5.<br><br>6.<br><br>**Your Physical Fitness**<br><br>1.<br><br>2.<br><br>3. |
|---|---|---|
|  | Check on the decided sub-goals every day, in the following manner |  |
|  | Follow-up check for practice thrice daily for 10 days – morning, afternoon, night |  |
|  | Follow-up check for practice twice daily for 10 days – morning, night |  |

|  | Follow-up check for practice once daily for 10 days, at night |  |
|---|---|---|

You can develop as many similar charts as you want, including one for use at work, at home, in your business, in your studies, or for any exam preparations.

Build your foundation as firmly as you can. The stronger you build your foundation, the better your chances of obtaining sustainable success. If you follow all the practices that I have mentioned in the book with inner discipline, you will find that you have blazed a path open for yourself. There may be others who may have relied on people like their parents or Godfathers to hew down the brambles and cut out a path for them to follow. However, when you instill all the qualities I have stressed in this book, you will become the master of your fate. You will become your own guide, coach, and mentor.

You will not need to rely on any Godfather to give you advice or help you ascend the peaks of success. I remember another famous story. It is the tale of a man who wanted to realize his dream. When he wanted to make his dream a reality, he was struck with a problem. He found that he did not possess enough strength or the means to succeed in this quest. He was clueless as to what to do next. Then he saw his father who seemed to have achieved some success in his life. He decided to consult his father. He asked his father, "Father, I want to achieve my dream. But I need your guidance.

Please help me!" His father was perplexed. He replied, "My dear son, there would be nothing in this world that would make me happier than helping you realize your dream. However, even I am not sure of how to help you. Whatever I know and have, I have already given you."

The son was disappointed with that response. He did not know what to do next. Then he heard that a wise man had come to his town. His countenance brightened as he thought that the wise man would have an answer for his problems. So, he went to meet the wise man. When he obtained an audience, he asked the wise man, "Dear master. Please enlighten me. Where can I find the strength to achieve my dreams?" The wise man looked out the window, pondering.

He then replied, "Someone once told me that the answer lay in the greatest heights of heaven. So, I climbed Mount Everest, the highest point on Earth to find the answer. However, when I went there, I found naught but freezing winds. When I came down the mountain, I realized that I had lost my precious time in that quest." The man was stumped when even the wise man could not provide him with the answer.

He then heard of a saint who resided in a place, a few towns over. He decided to seek him out to see if he could give him the answer. So, he boarded a bus and went to meet the saint. He asked him, "Oh, holy saint! What is the secret to achieving my dreams? Where can I find the strength to accomplish them?" The saint was a picture of serenity. He calmly answered, "You will find it in your prayers, Son. When you pray about your problems, you will find peace in your prayers even if your dreams are false." The saint then moved on. However, it only left the protagonist of the story even more confused. The message seemed coded and too esoteric for his liking. He found no answers to his questions. He sought many people to find the answer.

He found the answers given to him to be even more confusing. He had received a mishmash of opinions, but there was not one that he could use. He started muttering feverishly every day. He was walking down the road when an old man stopped him. His face was kind and his eyes seemed warm. He looked at the man and asked, "Why do you appear so confused and lost?" The man told him, "I have a dream. I want to achieve it and I feel that I do not have the strength to do so. I have asked many people to help me find that strength.

However, their answers have not provided me with any insight at all." The old man smiled and a light flashed in his eyes. He asked, "No one? Are you sure?" When the man nodded that he was, the old man asked him the most important question: "Did you ask yourself?"

This is the question you should pose yourself. When you have a dream to achieve, ask yourself. You have the potential within you. You have an inner Godfather who will not lead you astray. However, we have made his voice faint as we look outward for strength and guidance. Listen to yourself closely, and you will find that you will have the answers to your quest.

## The Final Bottom Line

In your pursuit to develop yourself and become sustainably successful, you must always remember that the most important parameter for you to develop upon is to be a good human being. When you look at all the chapters covered here, they invariably lead you to become a good human being first. In your ladder to success, never underestimate the most important things in your life, as described in this small piece:

Imagine that you are juggling five balls. Each of them represents important parts of our life – family, health, spirit, friends, and job. Four balls are made of glass, and only one is made of rubber.

We need to recognize that our work or our job is a rubber ball. While family, friends, health, and spirit are the other very fragile balls made up of glass. So, if you drop one of them, they will be irreversibly damaged or even shattered, while the rubber ball (job, work) will always bounce back. This understanding will help to keep the balance in your life.

Hence, while on your path to success, you may feel demotivated at times, and face a lot of failures too, but you will always bounce back like the rubber ball does; whereas, if you compromise on the glass balls, and if they break, they are broken forever and will never return to their former shape.

Therefore, always value what or who you have. At the same time, continue your work to attain success as well, maintaining the ideal work-life balance. You must also remember that anyone can attain one-time success. However, sustainable success cannot be forced upon or purchased because it is priceless.

Look up the story of any successful leader (I am not talking of dictators) from contemporary history who not only succeeded, but also remained successful, that is, they achieved sustainable success.

In each case, you will realize that they had a good heart. They were good human beings and hence moved up the ladder of success. They remained successful only on the basis of their hard work, strong base, determination, focus, passion, diligence, responsibility, humility, etc., and they achieved sustainable success that lasted for a long time, rather for the rest of their lives.

The main thing that is common between these successful leaders from the past and you in the present is that each one is a simple human being first. And if they could do it, why can you not?

There is absolutely no reason why you cannot do this.

You just need to start, now.

# ABOUT THE AUTHOR

Dr Kousar A Shah is a well-respected name in the healthcare leadership circuit. He has the reputation of being a 'turn around man' and a 'transformational leader' across the healthcare business world.

He is a medical doctor, a pediatrician, and a specialist in healthcare business management. He is a strategist and a hardcore process-oriented leader, having excellent people management skills, who enjoys building strong teams. He believes in and has created leaders with his training, experience, and teachings.

Though born to a well-reputed and honest High Court Judge, Dr Kousar A Shah faced many challenges right from his childhood as his father passed away early in his life. He and his family faced several challenges, including financial issues. Dr Kousar A Shah had no Godfather to guide him through his medical college days to his professional life and then shaping his professional career. He has lived on the inner callings, his innermost Godfather. He believes that one must develop the inner worth to succeed, rather than searching for outside support to attain truly long-lasting, sustainable success.

www.ingramcontent.com/pod-product-compliance
Lightning Source LLC
Chambersburg PA
CBHW022356040426
42450CB00005B/210